Breed Standard for the Bichon Havanese

D1365772

TAIL
Set high, thick at the base, tapering to a point as it curves over the rump like a plume, without touching the body.

HINDQUARTERS
Solidly muscular thighs with a convex outer edge. Viewed from the rear, the legs are perfectly straight and strongly boned with slightly angled joints. The hindquarters are covered with profuse, undulating hair.

COLOUR
Any colour or combination of colours is acceptable.

HEIGHT
Ranging from 23 to 30 cms (9 to 12 ins) at the withers; the ideal being 27 cms (10.5 ins).

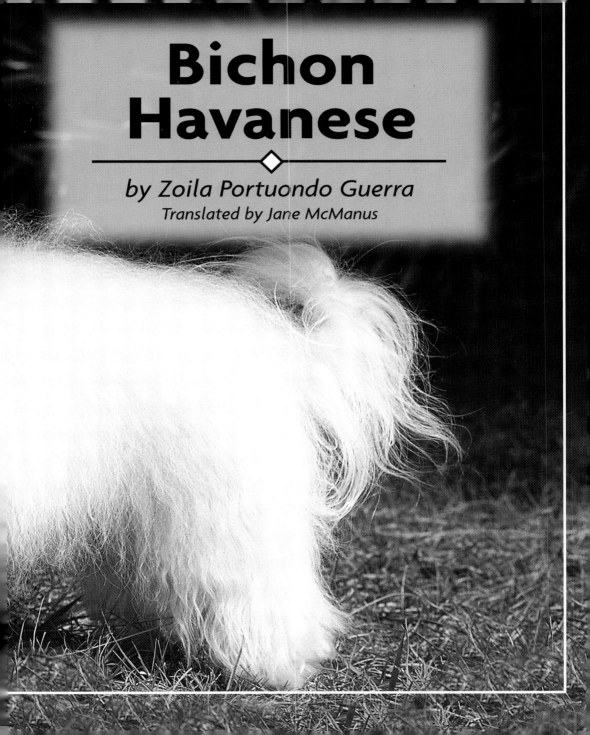

Bichon Havanese

by Zoila Portuondo Guerra
Translated by Jane McManus

Table of Contents

9

30

Origins of the Bichon Havanese

Meet the only existing purebred dog of Cuba, the Bichon Havanese, a member of the ancient family of Bichons and the favoured choice of the wealthy and educated of Havana. Map the breed's spreading popularity around the world, to the Continent and North America.

43

Personality and Characteristics of the Bichon Havanese

Take home the most personable and loving of all dogs, the Bichon Havanese, prized by Cubans for its intelligence, natural beauty and affectionate ways and becoming a companion of choice in many nations around the world.

Description of the Bichon Havanese

Learn the requirements of a well-bred Bichon Havanese by studying the description of the breed, as well as photos and illustrations showing the correct breed type.

48

Your Puppy Bichon Havanese

Be advised about choosing a reputable breeder and selecting a healthy, typical Havanese puppy. Understand the responsibilities of ownership and explore all aspects of caring for the new member of your family.

DISTRIBUTED BY:

PetLove™

Vincent Lane, Dorking
Surrey RH4 3YX
England

74

Photo Credits:

Herbert R. Axelrod
Norvia Behling
Carolina Biological Supply
Sandra Block
Doskocil
Isabelle Francais
Tony George
Zoila Potuondo Guerra
James Hayden-Yoav
James R. Hayden, RBP

Alice van Kempen
Dwight R. Kuhn
Dr. Dennis Kunkel
Mikki Pet Products
Phototake
Jean Claude Revy
Nikki Sussman
Theo von Sambeek
C. James Webb

Illustrations by Renée Low

98

123

150

A 'fleecy' wonder from Havana, the Bichon Havanese belongs to the Bichon family that dates back to the Renaissance.

HISTORY OF THE
Bichon Havanese

THE BICHON FAMILY

Before you read the particular history of the Bichon Havanese, you should know that this breed belongs to the family of dogs called Bichons, who were known throughout Europe for many centuries.

The French word Bichon means 'fleecy dog' and is thought to be a contraction of the word *Barbichon*, or 'bearded.' It is probably related to the French word *Barbet*, which is an ancient breed of water spaniel similar to the Poodle, from which all the Bichons of the world are descended. With time and use, the term Bichon has become synonymous with a dog completely covered with hair with a delightful people-oriented personality. In cynology circles, the term Bichon is applied to a group of dog breeds whose distant ancestors are the same. Bichon-type dogs have a long ancestry. References indicate they were known in ancient Greece. Some centuries later, they appeared in all the countries of the Mediterranean Basin and became very fashionable in Europe during the Renaissance. In the fifteen and sixteen centuries, they were introduced to other parts of the world through the expansion of the Spanish Empire that dominated Middle Europe at that time. The Spanish used their maritime power to conquer and colonise much of the New World, as well as some parts of Asia and Africa. It was said of Charles V, Hapsburg Holy Roman Emperor and King of

Unlike many of the other Bichon breeds, the Havanese appears in many colours and combination of colours, all of which are acceptable. This is Tammylan Marti.

Spain, that he presided over an empire so vast the sun never set on it.

Thanks to this dispersion of Bichons over many parts of the world during the sixteenth century, we now have a number of perfectly developed and defined breeds. In some of these countries, Bichons were mixed with other similar-type breeds and the outcome was different breeds with new images all their own. Different cultures and tastes produced different dogs such as the following breeds.

BICHON MALTESE
Its long white coat hangs evenly down each side of the body, which measures no more than 25 cms tall at the withers. This breed was described in 200 BC under the Latin name *Canis Melitaeus*, which could have referred to the island of Malta or the Sicilian town of Melita, and was concentrated in Italy. The Maltese is the tiniest of the Bichons and weighs less than 7 pounds, usually 4 to 6 pounds.

BICHON FRISE
Exclusively white and somewhat larger than the Maltese, its coat is frisé or curly, and shaped to the body. It is traced to the Bichon Teneriffe of the Canary Islands but was developed in Belgium and France. Like the Maltese, the Bichon

This pet Havanese, named Fama, was photographed in Cuba. Although not as glamourous as many of the show dogs, the pet Havaneses have terrific, loving personalities.

The Maltese is counted amongst the world's most glorious and glamorous breeds. Its silky floor length coat drapes luxuriously over its 4- to 6-pound body. This is an American champion Maltese.

As puppies, the Bichon breeds are astoundingly similar. This snow white trio is Bichon Maltese. Notice that the dark pigmentation on the eye rims and noses is already developing.

Unlike the Havanese that is presented in the show ring in its 'natural' coat, the Maltese is presented with its full-length coat groomed to perfection.

Frise has many admirers all over the world not just in its native land. The breed is medium sized, considered a Toy breed in Britain, though not so in America. The breed stands 9 to 11 inches high.

The curly Bichon breed, the Bichon Frise is the most popular Bichon breed in Britain as well as France and Belgium. It is the largest of the family of Bichons.

BICHON BOLOGNESE

Somewhat more square in shape than the other Bichons, the Bolognese has a flocked coat and is named for the area where it first made its mark, Bologna, Italy. Like the Maltese and Bichon Frise, the Bichon Bolognese is a solid white dog without markings of any kind. The breed stands 10 to 12 inches high.

LÖWCHEN

The Löwchen is a small, square dog of varied colours with a straight coat clipped to give it the appearance of a lion, thus giving the breed the name Little Lion Dog. It was known in Germany, France and Spain in the sixteenth century and is now considered a rare breed, although it has attracted attention on both sides of the Atlantic. Like the Havanese, the Löwchen can come in many colours not just the traditional white. In size,

The snow white powderpuff we call the Bichon Frise possesses a prominent head, slightly rounded, with 'halos' around its eyes. Of all the Bichon breeds, this dog has the most distinctive head.

The Bichon Frise is another Bichon breed that derived from dogs indigenous to an island, in this case the Canary Islands.

the Löwchen can stand 10 to 13 inches and weigh 8 to 18 pounds.

COTON DE TULEAR

The little-known Bichon of Madagascar derived from the same Bichon stock that arrived on the island of Tenerife, whence came the Bichon Frise. In French, *coton* means 'cotton' and describes the breeds desired coat type. The Coton de Tulear was recognised by the FCI in 1970, though the breed had been a favourite of French nobles in the seventeenth century. The breed stands 10 to 12 inches high. In colour, the breed is mainly white, though it can have champagne markings on the head and body. Some examples come in black and white.

ORIGINS OF THE BICHON HAVANESE

The Bichon Havanese originated in Cuba from an earlier breed known as Blanquito de la Habana. This white dog with a 'geographic' last name undoubtedly came from the famous port that was visited over centuries by ships and crews from all parts of the world including those bringing Spanish products, people and customs. All of them were welcomed by the warmth of Havana.

Cotton is this Bichon's calling card. The Coton de Tulear is a French breed, recognised by the FCI and the Kennel Club of England.

The Löwchen is a Bichon clipped to resemble a lion.

Bred from similar stock to the well-known Poodle, the Portuguese Water Dog shares many of the same characteristics, including a water-proof coat.

15

The Havanese on Cuba's largest tobacco plantation owned by the world-famous Alejandro Robaina, the only living person after whom a cigar is named. The Robaina Vega dates back to 1845 in Havana. Here Dr. Herbert Axelrod visits with Sr Robaina and his Havanese.

(FACING PAGE:) As young puppies, the Bichon breeds all appear adorable and furry! These two pups are Coton de Tulear.

A Cuban postage stamp celebrating the nation's only extant purebred dog: the Bichon Havanese.

look at history. When the Spaniards came to Cuba, they brought certain dogs that were useful to them in the colonisation process: Mastiffs and Spanish Bloodhounds and Greyhounds. They were big, strong dogs that could hunt, protect property and, when necessary, fight. These weren't the only dogs in Spain, however, and once the epoch of conquest gave way to a more stabilised colonial life, the Spaniards began to bring to the island smaller companion dogs to be enjoyed in the intimate life of the family.

Bichons had become a fashionable lapdog in Europe during the Renaissance, perhaps a little earlier. They were 'very small...very

The Bichon Havanese adorned and enlivened the homes of aristocratic Cubans during the eighteenth and nineteenth centuries. At the turn of the twentieth century, due to changes in fashion, taste, interests and influences, the Bichon Havanese was dismissed from the mansion but readily accepted in more modest homes.

To understand how all this happened, however, we have to take a closer

17

charming and alert...with hair so soft it seems like silk...bred by dames and nobles for their entertainment because of the tricks and games they were capable of learning and performing.' This description occurs in Victor Manuel Patiño's *Plantas Cultivadas y Animales Domésticos en la América Equinoccial.*

What better distraction on an island like Cuba, which was extremely isolated from Spain during the first two centuries of colonisation! The voyage sometimes could take as long as six months. The Cubans, of course, were anxious to keep abreast of the most refined European customs. In those days, Spain maintained a fierce commercial monopoly over Cuba, and it is probable that the first lapdogs to reach the island came directly from Spain or, via Spain, from other lands that had contact with the country.

Because of this monopoly, as well as the efforts of other European powers to grab the wealth of the Americas, Cuba carried on what has been termed a 'ransom trade' with French, English and Dutch pirates. Through these trades, both sides—pirates and colonists—acquired much of what they couldn't otherwise get in legal trade. It is not impossible that these contacts

introduced some lapdogs into Cuba, especially at the end of the seventeenth century.

All this leads to the conclusion that the most remote origins of the Bichon Havanese go back to the Spanish water dogs and Bichon-type lapdogs, although other Hispanic dogs of similar type may also have played a role. The Bichon brought from Europe to Cuba adapted to the island's particular diet and climate and to the customs and tastes of the residents. Eventually, these conditions gave birth to a different dog, smaller than its predecessors, with a completely white coat of a silkier texture closer to the preferences and luxurious living conditions of its new breeders. This dog was the Blanquito de la Habana.

Many writers point to the early eighteenth century as the period when a dog that the British called 'White Cuban' was recognised in England with some fanfare. This Blanquito de la Habana or Perro de Seda de la Habana (Havanese Silk Dog), as it was later called, has erroneously been identified as the Bichon Havanese or the Bichon Maltese, and this has led to confusions and misconceptions.

Although little was printed in Cuba in that period, by the end of the eighteenth century, we find clear evidence that the Blanquito de la Habana had multiplied in the wealthy homes of Havana. One such testimony is that of the famous Countess of Merlin, a Cuban-born resident in France, in her *Viaje a la Habana* (Trip to Havana). She describes the typical gifts she received from her Cuban family before returning to France: '...two little dogs about six inches long, with large round black eyes that shine through long hair as white as snow, lie in baskets adorned with rose-colored ribbons awaiting the departure...' It is curious that this Cuban residing in France, who travelled in the most refined society of Paris and Madrid and must have had contact with European lapdogs, should con-

For years the Havanese has been confused with the original Cuban Bichon breed, the now extinct Blanquito de la Habana. Today's Havanese should not be referred to as a Havanese Silk Dog. This is the author with a bitch called Esmeralda de la Giraldilla, a Cuban champion.

sider the Blanquito de la Habana so unusual and typical of her native isle that she never compared it to any other breed.

Other evidence appears in 'Portrait of a Young Woman,' painted in 1797 by Cuba's first important painter, Vicente Escobar, whose subjects were upper-class Cubans. It shows an aristocratic young woman hold-

19

ing a Blanquito de la Habana in her arms. At the end of the eighteenth century, the *Papel Periódico de la Habana*, the island's most important daily

the Cuban landed gentry zealously followed refined European customs, imitating the latest fashions with surprising success. It was said that, in Havana, the upper classes dressed and lived like those in Madrid, London or Paris, and that Havana featured performances by the most famous European theatre and opera companies (for the rich, naturally). At the same time, living conditions on the island, the climate—so different from that of the Continent—as well as other factors had formed a Cuban character that was different from the peninsular character. Naturally, these cultural changes also affected dogs.

Three 'fine dogs' setting a new fashion trend in the canine world. For many years in Cuba, the Havanese was incorrectly called Maltese. The bitches above are (l to r) Dolly and Epoca de la Giraldilla, owned by the Carbonell family, and Esmeralda de la Giraldilla.

newspaper, carried notices of lost dogs and advertisements for 'fine dogs.' ('Fine dog' was synonymous with Maltese, the name that Cubans popularly and incorrectly applied to the Bichon Havanese, and still do.) In addition, a critical journal of 1800, El Regañon de la Habana, attacked the fashionable customs of the wealthy, such as the hours spent bathing and grooming their lapdogs.

The eighteenth century marked the beginning of the consolidation of Cuban tastes and styles, although much of

The Blanquito de la Habana was, like any other dog breed, a clear product of the taste and culture of its breeders, who imposed the seal of their period and circumstances. They preferred a miniature white dog, with long, silky hair and an extremely loving and lively character.

The *Diccionario Enciclopédico Hispano-americano*, published in 1894, described it as follows: 'the little Havanese dog, *Canis vellerosus*, exists in Havana; it is smaller [than the Maltese] and is covered with a type of fleece that is long, curly, white and satiny or silky. The specimens taken to Europe have been unable to resist the change of climate for very long'.

Finally, listen to the description of the Blanquito given by the Spanish writer Alejandro Bon in El Perro: 'It is a veritable snowball, or to put it better, a ball of white silk, with a black nose and lively, bright eyes almost hidden behind the long hair that hangs from its head. It is very small and weighs no more than two-and-a-half kilograms. Since its long hair falls to the ground, its feet are invisible and it seems to advance by dragging them. Its tail is like a plume, very fluffy, inclined over the back and to one side. It has a lively, intelligent character and, although it is very loyal to its masters, it can be somewhat disdainful on occasion. This dog requires constant bathing and special care in order to keep it healthy'.

J. Brouwer Etchecopar, a pioneer of cynological studies in Cuba, wrote the following in

As more and more European traditions were adopted in Cuba in the nineteenth century, the Cubans became enamored with the German and French Poodles, which were crossed with the existing Blanquito to create today's Bichon Havanese. Here, Esmeralda de la Giraldilla, owned by Merita Batista and Annia Barroso, is photographed in front of La Chorrera Castle in Havana.

Razas Caninas: 'There is considerable confusion concerning the Blanquito Cubano. According to Lloyd, it is a cross between a German or French Toy Poodle and a Maltese, but larger than the latter and with hair that touches the ground. The name Maltese is also somewhat confusing, for that is what this dog is called in the capital of Cuba, whereas in other European countries it is known as either Havanese or Blanquito de la Habana, and we haven't yet been able to unravel these anomalies.' The only problem here is that Lloyd and Etchecopar are no longer talking about the Blanquito de la Habana, but rather the Bichon

(FACING PAGE) The Poodle has been involved in the development of more breeds than any other dog. No wonder! Considered the height of fashion, elegance and athleticism, the Poodle contributed its intelligence, non-shedding coat and people-loving personality.

Havanese; and, although the two breeds belong to the Bichon family, their characteristics are notably different.

When Spain ended the trade monopoly in Cuba, the island began to enjoy the advantages that its privileged geographic position presented. Immigrants arrived on the island to work the fertile land and establish their businesses. The French are a case in point, particularly those who had lived in the French colonies of Santo Domingo and Haiti. When revolution erupted there, thousands

In the development of the Bichon Havanese, the Blanquito de la Habana was much more dominant than the Poodle.

of French settlers immigrated to Cuba, bringing not only their wealth but also their culture and their lifestyle, which naturally included their dogs.

Caniches or Poodles, likely originally from Germany but adopted by France, became known in nineteenth-century Cuba. Some may have arrived with the French immigrants, but their predecessors could also have come from Germany, via France, or from Spain itself, since these countries had a direct relationship with the breed.

With the arrival in Cuba of a greater number of Poodles, the Blanquito de la Habana began its transformation. It is not surprising that the Criollo landowners were somewhat bowled over by these new dogs and considered it advantageous to cross them with their native breed, perhaps with the idea of increasing the size and varying the colour of the Blanquito de la Habana. Thus, gradually, a new breed arrived on the scene: the Bichon Havanese.

The Bichon Havanese, then, originated in the nineteenth century as the result of mating Blanquitos de la Habana with Poodles. In this mating, it is evident that the type of the Bichon remain unaltered. In reality, the Cuban Poodle breeder has had to make every effort to eliminate from his lines the elongated body and short legs of the Bichon that were defini-

tively imposed in these early crosses, not only through genetics but through the traditionally cultivated taste that gave preference to this breed's phenotype.

Bred in Germany, this irresistible darling is Sandra Block's Brilliance Belissima. She couldn't be more beautiful.

In any case, the Bichon Havanese is, above all (and outside any hypotheses concerning its origin), the sum of a great variety of antecedents—as are Cuban people themselves. The Havanese is the Cuban interpretation of the Bichon lapdog so abundant in Europe since the Renaissance. Like the Blanquito de la Habana before it, the Bichon Havanese was the pet of the colonial aristocracy until the beginning of the twentieth century, when North American tastes were imposed, producing a change in canine fashion and preference. From that moment on, the Bichon Havanese was no longer the indulged mascot of the wealthy and became, instead, the daring and affectionate friend of the common people of the city.

It continued to be bred in Cuba all through the twentieth century (especially as a pet) because it remained the preferred dog of the Cuban family. The Havanese's character, so similar to that of its masters, the ease with which it can be handled, its extraordinary intelligence and its beautiful coat all contributed to the uninterrupted popularity of the breed as a family companion. During the last quarter of the twentieth century, however, its breeding has been notably increased and, it has become not just a companion but a valued show dog, enjoying great success because of its grace and happy disposition. During Cuba's all-breed dog shows of 1993 and 1994, two Bichons Havaneses won, respectively, the titles of Reserve Best in Show and Best Puppy in Show. Another pup of this breed also won the latter title in the 1997 all-breed show held in Havana.

For nearly a decade, the Bichon Havanese has been protected by its parent club, the Cuban Club of the Bichon Havanese (CCBH). Officially founded by the author in 1991, the CCBH established a rigor-

A famous male Havanese from Finland, is Cikitata Uno Gizmo. Havaneses have proven excellent show dogs in Cuba as well as on the Continent and in America.

ous genetic program designed to guarantee the correct development of the Bichon Havanese and set breeding lines under the affix 'de la Giraldilla,' which is the symbol of Havana. The CCBH is a member of the Federación Cinológica de Cuba, or Cuban Kennel Club, which, in turn, belongs to the Fédération Cynologique Internationale.

The popularity of this breed grows constantly in Cuba, its native country, where its profusion is in curious contrast to the scarcity of the Bichon Havanese in the rest of the world.

THE BICHON HAVANESE IN AMERICA

Cuba and the United States maintained a close relationship during the first half of the twentieth century. Given the number of Cubans who lived in the United States during the colonial period and the incidence of American residency on the island after that, the Bichon Havanese was probably known in the north from the turn of the century or before. Nevertheless, systematic breeding of the Bichon Havanese in the United States began only in the 1970s.

25

This happy Havanese is an American companion and show dog.

After the success of the Socialist Revolution in Cuba in the 1960s, many wealthy Cubans migrated from the island to the Southern United States and other nearby countries such as Puerto Rico and Costa Rica. Some of them took along their dogs, including the Bichon Havanese as a lively reminder of their native land. With time, these Cuban emigrants began to implant their culture and tastes in their new homeland—especially in Florida, where most of the Cuban refugees settled. Because of the numbers of Cubans, the impact of their customs and lifestyle on American society was much greater than ever before. Visiting Florida today, the Cuban influence is profound, both in culture and language.

The growing popularity of the Havanese in the United States can be attributed to the breed's endearing personality, its excellent health and its good looks.

This infusion of Cuban culture resulted in the fortunate situation in which a U.S. breeder named Dorothy Goodale learned of the existence of the Bichon Havanese. Intrigued and fascinated, Mrs Goodale began to seek more information on this canine breed she had never heard of before, one that offered an alternative to the big dogs she had preferred to breed when she was younger. She decided to advertise in a Miami paper in order to locate specimens of the little dog, and it was through these advertisements that she found two or three immigrant families who had brought their Bichons from Cuba to the United States. From them,

The Havanese has existed in America since the mid-1970s. As many Cubans have gone to the States to live, more and more interest in the Havanese has spread. This Havanese *señorita* is ready for a night on the town.

Mrs Goodale succeeded in acquiring six Bichons Havaneses with pedigrees: a bitch with four female pups and a young unrelated male. A little later, she was able to obtain five more males from a Cuban who was moving from Costa Rica to Texas and couldn't manage to maintain his canine family.

An experienced breeder, Mrs Goodale began working with the 11 Bichons she had obtained using the breed standard published by the Fédération Cynologique Internationale. Her first Bichon Havanese lines appeared in 1974 and were an immediate success in attracting other breeders. In 1979, Dorothy Goodale, with her husband Bert and a group of collaborators, founded the Havanese Club of America for those interested in breeding and owning a Bichon Havanese.

In 1991, the United Kennel Club in the U.S. announced its recognition of the Bichon Havanese and accepted any dogs registered by the Goodales. The Havanese Club of America was granted recognition from the American Kennel Club in 1996.

27

Meanwhile, the original club split. Dorothy Goodale and some friends reformed as the Original Havanese

Havaneses bred in the U.S. today differ significantly from the present-day Cuban dogs, though the type has improved steadily over the past decade.

Club of America, whilst the other group continued as the Havanese Club of America.

In developing her Bichon Havanese lines, Goodale followed the FCI standard approved in 1963, which recognised the breed as Cuban; but, with time, she considered it necessary to modify that breed standard and did so. Two standards now exist in the United States: that of the Original Havanese Club of America and that of the Havanese Club of America (which was probably written after the club split). The two are very similar and quite close to the Cuban standard. The

FCI and the English Kennel Club each have their own standards.

With the passage of time and the increased number of Bichons in the United States, breeders there began exporting them to Europe. Now the Bichon Havanese is known in various European countries and is rapidly gaining popularity, as much for its exoticism as for the qualities that make it not only a pretty show dog but also an excellent companion and watchdog.

It should be noted, however, that reproduction of the Bichon Havanese outside Cuba has somewhat weakened the homogeneity and correct type. After all, breeding in the United States began with a very limited genetic pool and this has been the case all along due to the impossibility of acquiring dogs originating in Cuba, the real base of the breed and an unlimited genetic pool.

This history of the Bichon Havanese in the United States ends on a positive note, for the breed is now recognised by the American Kennel Club, which is the guiding institution for breed dogs in the United States.

The Barbet of France is a poodle-like breed with a moderate following on the Continent. The Barbet is believed to be the forerunner of the Poodle, probably one of France's most ancient breeds. It is therefore a likely contributor to the Bichon breeds as well.

CHARACTERISTICS OF THE
Bichon Havanese

**THE FAMILY IS GROWING:
YOU NOW HAVE A
BICHON HAVANESE!**
So you've decided you want a
dog. Maybe you already know

what that means... maybe not.

If you've never had one of
these delightful animals, you
should know that a dog requires
your attention and effort. It needs
to be trained, bathed, groomed,
systematically wormed and vaccinated, occasionally treated by a
vet, regularly exercised and consistently loved. If you aren't willing to face all this, it's best to

think twice, because a live animal
is not a toy. Without proper care,
it can become a troublesome bur-
den instead of what a dog essentially is: a source of enjoyment,
affection and entertainment.

Let's assume, though, that
you're willing and ready...and
that you've just acquired a
Bichon Havanese. You won't
regret it, I assure you. The
Havanese is amazingly intelligent, lively, playful and very
devoted to its owners. It will
immediately show its affection
for you and yours (including the
children) and, from the moment
you bring it home, become a part
of family life.

Of course, you have to keep
in mind that this endearing little
dog is at its best when its coat is
correctly maintained and its body
and character are fully developed. A dog whose coat is dirty,
matted or clipped (for the convenience of owners who aren't prepared to devote the necessary
time to its grooming) is not a
pretty dog. With an adequate diet
and sufficient exercise, your pet
will develop the strong bones
and muscles that are characteris-
tic of a healthy, beautiful animal.

There can be no doubt that the Havanese is one of the world's most devoted companion animals. Havaneses live for your every word and gesture.

30

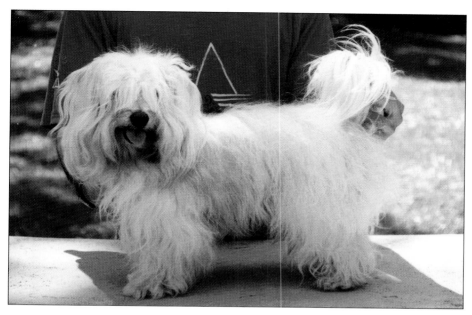

No home is complete without a Havanese! Do not take the commitment of a Havanese lightly. This dog thrives on your affection and positive energy.

Finally, a dog that is over-indulged, as well as one that is ignored or maltreated, will become either timid or aggressive and hence lose one of its finest features: its natural temperament.

You've taken on a responsibility, but don't be alarmed. You'll be rewarded with memorable moments; and probably you'll wind up like other owners of this breed, living with two, three or more Bichons Havaneses. You will also begin recommending them to all your friends and relatives.

CHARACTERISTICS
OF THE HAVANESE
OWNER CONSIDERATIONS
When you spoil your dog or stimulate its relatively strong charac-ter, you are lessening its delightful personality. The Bichon Havanese is born to live in your home and not in a patio or a kennel, but at the same time, this dog requires plenty of exercise because of its vitality and restlessness. Don't over-indulge your pet but don't maltreat or reprimand it either. Just let it be.

I have known owners who don't let their Havanese walk. These creatures love to be carried and caressed. Since they respond with appropriately endearing and picturesque gestures, many people can't resist their bewitching ways and wind up turning their Bichons into dolls that can't walk on a leash, much less enjoy a good run in the park. Be strong.

As beguiling and bewitching as the Bichon Havanese is, you must resist the temptation to spoil your dog. You can indeed 'spoil' your dog's temperament and reliability.

Don't let yourself be drawn in by their cajolery—for your own good and theirs.

Pet them, but not so constantly that they become clinging. Let them relate to other dogs and other people. Unless you have aggressive dogs or a big breed that can become a real threat to your Bichon, don't overprotect it from the others. It can take care of itself. If you become the protector, various problems can arise. Your Bichon Havanese will become timid, unable to get along with other dogs. Possibly, if you have an excellent-quality Havanese, on the day you decide to mate it, you'll find that it rejects its mate with indifference or aggression. This is especially important in males. When they are over-socialised with people and don't know how to relate to

other dogs, they can't adequately express their virile tendencies.

It really isn't good for a dog to live alone, isolated from other dogs. Even after centuries of domestication and a very close relationship with humans—whom your dog will consider a part of his pack—the dog develops his personality only in relation to his fellow creatures. Moreover, other dogs can alleviate his solitude and permit him to communicate fully in his 'own language.' You probably recall times when you have felt like a fish out of water, perhaps in a foreign country where you had to communicate in another language and adapt to other customs. It was all very interesting, but remember how comfortable it felt to return home, to be able to talk and act naturally? The same thing happens to animals that live only with humans. If the humans know nothing about the language and body signals of dogs, trying to make their dogs understand their own language, it is even more difficult for the dogs. Then, too, dogs have needs that we, as humans, repress rather than understand and satisfy. This is the case with pups that need to chew and, when they destroy their masters' furniture or shoes, they're banned or abandoned. We don't understand that a dog acts that way because it feels alone or because it is teething and has to chew. Neither do we understand that a pup plays with our shoes because he likes the scent of the owner. Since our shoes smell strongly of 'us', the dog feels consoled and secure by chewing on them whilst he is alone.

Your Havanese, with a character all its own, does the things he does for good reason. Owners must make a special effort to

Whilst everyone has perfectly justifiable reasons for loving and adoring their own dog, not every dog is suitable for breeding. Not only can breeding your Havanese be very costly and time-consuming, it can also be very dangerous for the dam (and puppies).

Breeding dogs is a matter for professionals. The breeder must be knowledgeable, first of all

Havaneses can make excellent watchdogs and babysitters for your children. Be wary: children must be instructed how to handle the Havanese. It is cruel to allow children to grab and maul the Havanese's hair, ears and limbs.

understand and appreciate their dogs. Don't forget that the Bichon Havanese is an intelligent dog, always ready and able to learn new things.

BREEDING YOUR HAVANESE

So many of us are so enamoured of our own Havanese that it seems imperative that we breed them. 'Who wouldn't want a Havanese exactly like mine?'

about the breeding lines they're working. We must know the breed standard thoroughly and the faults and virtues of the specimens involved in the mating. We have to know how to fix desirable traits and eliminate undesirable traits; and, naturally, we have to be very clear about our objective. In a word, the breeder needs a good head and a good eye.

Let's suppose, though, that

33

Born in Havana! Bebita de la Giraldilla, owned by Merita Batista, with her litter. Note that the puppies are born blind and smooth coated. Whelping a litter is a huge responsibility that should not be assumed by novices.

What could be cuter than a Havanese puppy? Raising young puppies requires constant attention by the breeder and dam. Like human infants, puppies are dependent on you for everything!

you don't pretend to be a breeder but that you have an excellent-quality Havanese whom you believe is worthy of reproducing. Your bitch is 18 months old and in her third heat cycle. You have made the decision before your female came into heat so that you could evaluate her physical faults and virtues as well as her temperament. It is always helpful to study your dog's siblings, parents and grandparents so that you have some idea of the genetic material available. Undoubtedly, you took time to visit a number of males in order to determine which would be the best option for your female.

The male should be essentially masculine, well developed, healthy and well fed. It should be active and self-confident. A timid, nervous dog is a defective dog as far as mating is concerned. You want to mate only healthy specimens with good temperaments. You also want to select for your female a male that is satisfactory or better in the features in which she is deficient. In a word, choose the best male available, the one most representative of the breed type. Make sure he is free of genetic diseases. If possible, try to meet some of his off-

This six-month-old debutante is A Maiden Effort's Funny Face, owned by German breeder Sandra Block.

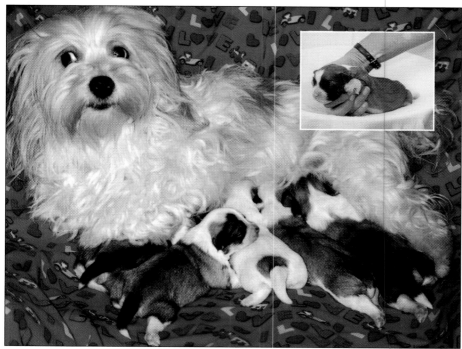

At five days old, these Havanese babies are suckling from their mother, Beryll.

spring in order to have an idea of what he is producing. Then, and then only, contract with his owner for the mating.

In a general sense, females that are physically and mentally prepared for maternity make good reproducers. Those with a placid temperament and a mater-

years, whilst the ideal age for breeding is between 2 and 5 years.

The best way to arrange the mating is by written contract stating the conditions . Either you can pay a stud fee or permit the owner of the male to select one or more pups, depending

Winning in the show ring is the universally accepted way of proving breeding value. A champion Havanese will be greatly in demand as a sire for suitable bitches. This prize-winning sire is Cikitata Uno Gizmo of Finland.

nal nature combined with correct conformation are best. Nervous and excitable females, those that are very small and, of course, those with physical defects are not recommended.

The ideal age for the first birth is between 15 months and 3

on the size of the litter. Get advice from an experienced breeder on this matter and on the choice of the stud.

Usually, the owner of the bitch takes her to the home of the stud, where all the conditions for this visit have been previously coordinated to facilitate the mating. This means that, as soon as the bitch is in heat, her owner should advise the owner of the stud to specify the date of mating.

The reproduction cycle of female dogs normally occurs twice a year and the symptoms are inflammation of the vulva and bleeding, which continues for about ten days. When bleeding stops, the moment for mating arrives. In any case, it's best to consult your veterinarian so that everything turns out the way you want.

The site of the mating should be a tranquil, isolated spot where the dogs won't be overexcited by outside stimuli. Two matings on different days are ideal. Real coupling occurs when the dogs are physically joined end to end for between 10 and 30 minutes.

The gestation period ranges from 59 to 64 days, which makes it vitally important to record the exact dates of the matings. In that way, you will know the probable day of birth and be able to prepare for it properly.

When your bitch is ready to give birth, find her a quiet place where she can be alone and where you can watch her. If you lack experience in these matters, keep in touch with your vet before and during birth.

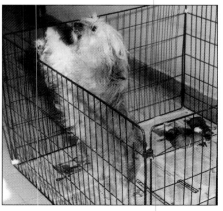

Whelping and rearing a litter is hard work for the dam too! She has to attend to her litter 24 hours a day for 10 to 12 weeks. Don't neglect the dam's needs: she will still need attention, a special diet and ample opportunity for exercise (away from the litter).

Generally, the mother births her pups by herself without any problem, but certain factors may have a negative influence, such as: fussing and handling by her owners, noise and movement in the birthing area, small pelvic capacity or very big pups. There are cases where the bitch births her pups surrounded by the family, which can make her nervous to the point of inhibiting the birth.

Don't permit her to give birth on rags or cloths. It is better to use old newspapers that can be changed constantly as the birth continues. Cloths are not suitable because the pups can become tangled and suffocate in them.

Puppies in their first week of life do little more than sleep and eat. The breeder must take care that all the puppies are nursing sufficiently and that the dam isn't neglecting any particular baby.

Once the birth is over, watch the mother discreetly. Keep her where she's quiet and within sight. Sometimes, without meaning to, the mother will lie down on a pup and asphyxiate it; or she might decide to move the pups to another and less appropriate spot, such as under the bed. Make sure the mother has milk and that all the pups are nursing normally. A healthy Havanese litter is cause for celebration. The breeder's hard work and preparation reap wonderful furry rewards. The proud breeder in Havana passes out only the best cigars upon the whelping of a beautiful litter of puppies. (That's a distinct advantage of the Havanese!)

The average Havanese litter is three or four pups, although litters of six or even seven are not uncommon. The puppy's colour at birth is seldom the same as when it reaches adulthood for, with the exception of white or light beige, the colour will probably be diluted. Black pups, for example, often grow up to be grey, whilst brown or red pups may turn out to be beige or ivory. A black and white pup may remain the same or become grey and white. The matter of colour is genetic, of course. Nevertheless, a Havanese breeder should not breed for colour, but rather for soundness, conformation and temperament. Though useful in relation to pigmentation, colour is only an aesthetic element and does not determine the dog's quality.

This is not the place to go into detail about raising pups. We simply want to note that, after three weeks, you can begin to give the little ones solid food in order to help the mother wean them and teach them how to eat. The vet can recommend the appropriate food, indicate when and how to

At eight weeks of age, this litter seems fairly ready to take on the world. This is the first litter bred by breeder Sandra Block of Germany.

worm them and, later, vaccinate them properly according to age.

Most importantly, we urge you not to reproduce dogs capriciously. Before you even think of mating your dog, determine whether its pups will have the future they deserve. Mate exclusively with those specimens that can reproduce quality. Any other course will be a detriment to the development of the breed you appreciate so much.

Life is a privilege. A dog is a marvellous form of life. For many centuries, this creature has been our friend and confidante, showering us with loyalty and love without asking whether we really deserve it, accepting us as we are without judging us. All this is much more than we can ever expect of another human being.

Having a Bichon Havanese is a highly gratifying and healthy experience. Science has documented over and over again the beneficial effects pets have on our physical and mental health. For this reason the Bichon Havanese is one of the breeds used in therapy work in the United States. Owners of Havanese bring their dogs to nursing homes and rest facilities to visit the sick and aged. The Havanese brighten the spirit of thousands of people around the world.

A dog is also a lesson for any attentive owner who allows himself to be influenced by his pet's natural wisdom. We should be able to treat him as he treats us. Never maltreat him. Don't neglect him. And, above all do not abandon him.

A Bichon Havanese can establish such a close link with his human friend that it's sometimes hard to tell who's who in this relationship. And he may not be able to survive being separated from the owner he loves. For that reason, we have to think carefully before we decide to acquire a dog. A dog is a responsibility we cannot reject under any circumstances. 'We are responsible for what we domesticate,' said Saint-Exupéry's Little Prince, and he was right.

Your Havanese is a remarkable gift! Never take your dog for granted. Be firm in your commitment to own a Havanese, and give him the best life you can.

40

Make your Havanese a part of your life. Provide fun opportunities to exercise and socialise for your dog. He will become a more well-rounded and loving companion. The author and two other owners are walking their dogs on the Malacon, a popular thoroughfare in Havana. The sea is to the left.

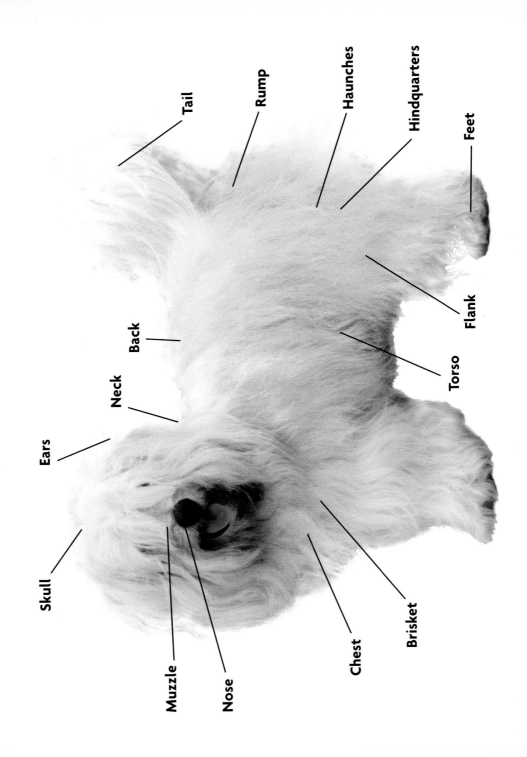

Tail

Rump

Haunches

Hindquarters

Feet

Back

Flank

Neck

Torso

Ears

Skull

Chest

Brisket

Muzzle

Nose

DESCRIPTION OF THE
Bichon Havanese

The Bichon Havanese is a companion dog and is classified in Group IX by the Fédération Cynologique Internationale (FCI). The FCI is an organisation that promotes the breeding and showing of purebred dogs around the world. The following description gives the ideal representative of the Bichon Havanese. The breed standard is the measuring stick by which breeders breed and judges judge. For the average pet owner, the standard gives all the important features that the breed should possess, from body type and colour to coat texture and temperament.

WHAT THE BICHON HAVANESE SHOULD LOOK LIKE
HEAD
The head is proportional to the size of the body, with a broad, flattened skull and moderate nasal-frontal depression. The muzzle is slightly longer than the forehead and the stop is moderate but perfectly visible. Its large, dark, expressive, almond-shaped eyes are surrounded by a halo of pigmentation. The nose is pronounced, tapered and black; the mouth is ample with fine, black

lips. The underjaw is flat and firm. Teeth meet in a scissors bite. The medium-sized ears are broad-based and implanted slightly above eye level. They fall to a point without covering the cheeks. The ears have a slight dip that rises when the dog is at attention, giving this breed its unusual look of alertness. Long hair falls from the occiput over the muzzle, covering the eyes, which are barely visible behind this sunshade.

The head should be broad with a flat skull, adorned with long hair, creating a sunshade over the eyes— ideal for a dog living in sunny Cuba.

NECK
Moderately long and erect, with no dewlap.

The body should be somewhat longer than tall. The torso is covered with long, silky hair.

BODY
The Bichon Havanese is somewhat longer than it is tall. The flanks are firm and rounded, the haunches high and the back strong, with the spine sloping slightly toward the rump. The sternum line coincides with elbow height. The torso is covered with abundant, silky hair—often 4 inches long in this zone and a little longer on the chest than on the stomach—which never reaches the ground.

FOREQUARTERS
Short, straight and moderately angled. Longitude from feet to elbows is the same as from elbows to withers. Leg bones are strong, feet rounded and the hair is shorter here than on the torso.

HINDQUARTERS
Solidly muscular thighs with a convex outer edge. Viewed from the rear, the legs are perfectly straight and strongly boned with moderately angled joints. The feet are oval-shaped. The hindquarters are covered with profuse, undulating hair.

TAIL
Set high, the tail is thick at the base and tapers to a point as it curves over the rump like a plume, without touching the body. If the tail is too close to the body or curly, it destroys the harmony and correct image of the Bichon Havanese, especially its walk.

SKIN
Tight to the body, wrinkle-free and cream-coloured.

COAT
The beauty of the Bichon Havanese is in its coat, which should be abundant over the entire body. The hair is fine, long and undulating, with a very typical pearly sheen. The hair on the paws is shorter than on the body.

COLOUR
Any colour or combination of colours is acceptable in the Bichon Havanese, though, as we have already noted, the most common colours are ivory or champagne.

A young Cuban Havanese puppy named Magico, shaping up nicely for the show ring. The puppy coat is replaced by the adult coat by around eight months of age. This puppy's coat will become lighter as he matures.

HEIGHT

Height at the withers can range from 23 to 30 centimetres (9 to 12 inches), but the ideal is 27 centimetres (10.5 inches).

MOVEMENT

The Bichon Havanese should move freely and easily, with a lively, elegant gait. The head is held high and the tail movement conveys will and pride.

FAULTS

Incorrect bite: overshot, undershot or clamp bite. Crooked bones. Poor pigmentation. Corkscrew tail. Timidity.

The Havanese standard does not make a smile mandatory, but it sure does reveal the breed's joy of life.

45

CHARACTER

The temperament of the Bichon Havanese plays a decisive role in its form. These dogs should be neither timid nor aggressive. By character, the breed is lively, intelligent and up to any situation. It shows no cowardice, in spite of its size. It enjoys sharing with its family every kind of inside or outside activity, from swimming, running to romping in the grass or in the snow. Its joy in life and its sense of innate pride are clearly expressed in its movements and in how it carries its head and tail. It gets along well with others of the same breed and even other breeds; for, although the Bichon Havanese is somewhat dominant, it's not a quarrelsome dog.

The breed standard describes the Havanese's unusual look of alertness as well as its innate pride and vivacity, evident in the breed's carriage and movement.

The skull is broad and flat and the muzzle is slanted back, with a perfectly visible stop.

The eyes are dark and almond shaped, surrounded by dark pigmentation.

The nose is entirely black, without blotchy pink pigmentation (Dudley nose).

The body and head are profusely covered with long silky hair, giving the dog a natural, 'ungroomed' appearance. The tail curves up like a plume.

The longitude from feet to elbows is the same as from elbows to withers. The hair on the chest is longer than on the stomach.

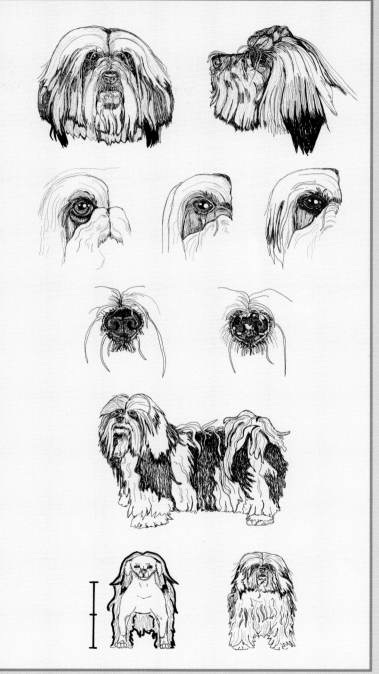

Bichon Havanese

WHERE TO BEGIN?

If you are convinced that the Bichon Havanese is the ideal dog for you, it's time to learn about where to find a puppy and what to look for. We recommend very seriously to anyone interested in acquiring a Bichon Havanese outside Cuba that he investigate the breeder's bloodlines for possible genetic diseases, of which progressive retinal atrophy (PRA) and cataracts are great concerns. Responsible breeders screen their dogs for these possible problems and never include an affected dog or possible carrier in their breeding programme. Whether you are seeking a pet dog or show dog, freedom from genetic diseases is of paramount importance. Both PRA and cataracts can lead to blindness in an afflicted Havanese. You will find it useful, when looking for a Bichon Havanese, to listen to the opinion of registries that have lists of dogs that are clear of certain genetic diseases.

Locating a litter of Bichons Havaneses hopefully should not present a problem for the new owner. Although this is a relatively new breed in Britain, with a moderate following on the Continent and in America, you should be able to locate reputable breeders within a reasonable distance of your home. You are looking for an established breeder

DID YOU KNOW?

Unfortunately, when a puppy is bought by someone who does not take into consideration the time and attention that dog ownership requires, it is the puppy who suffers when he is either abandoned or placed in a shelter by a frustrated owner. So all of the 'homework' you do in preparation for your pup's arrival will benefit you both. The more informed you are, the more you will know what to expect and the better equipped you will be to handle the ups and downs of raising a puppy. Hopefully, everyone in the household is willing to do his part in raising and caring for the pup. The anticipation of owning a dog often brings a lot of promises from excited family members: 'I will walk him every day,' 'I will feed him,' 'I will housebreak him,' etc., but these things take time and effort, and promises can easily be forgotten once the novelty of the new pet has worn off.

Be certain that your breeder has screened his stock for eye problems. Your puppy should have dark, clear eyes.

with outstanding dog ethics and a strong commitment to the breed. New owners should have as many questions as they have doubts. An established breeder is indeed the one to answer your four million questions and make you comfortable with your choice of the Bichon Havanese. An established breeder will sell you a puppy at a fair price if, and only if, the breeder determines that you are a suitable, worthy owner of his/her dogs. An established breeder can be relied upon for advice, no matter what time of day or night. A reputable breeder will accept a puppy back, without questions, should you decide that this not the right dog for you.

Choosing a breeder is an important first step in

DID YOU KNOW?
Your selection of a good puppy can be determined by your needs. A show potential or a good pet? It is your choice. Every puppy, however, should be of good temperament. Although show-quality puppies are bred and raised with emphasis on physical conformation, responsible breeders strive for equally good temperament. Do not buy from a breeder who concentrates solely on physical beauty at the expense of personality.

DID YOU KNOW?
You should not even think about buying a puppy that looks sick, undernourished, overly frightened or nervous. Sometimes a timid puppy will warm up to you after a 30-minute 'let's-get-acquainted' session.

dog ownership. Fortunately, the majority of Bichon Havanese breeders are devoted to the breed and its well being. The Kennel Club is able to recommend breeders of quality Bichons Havaneses, as can any local all-breed club or Bichon Havanese club. Potential owners are encouraged to attend a dog show to view the Bichons Havaneses in the fur, to see what Havaneses look like outside of a photographer's lens. Provided you approach the handlers when they are not terribly busy with the dogs, most are more than willing to answer questions, recommend breeders and give advice.

Now that you have contacted and met a breeder or two and made your choice about which breeder is best suited to your needs, it's time to visit the litter. Keep in mind that many quality breeders have waiting lists. Sometimes new owners have to wait as long as two years for a puppy. If you are really committed to the breeder whom you've selected, then you will wait (and

In Spanish, we call puppies *perritos* or *cachorros!* These three are only three weeks old.

hope for an early arrival!). If not, you may have to resort to your second or third choice breeder. Don't be too anxious, however. If the breeder doesn't have any waiting list, or any customers, there is probably a good reason. Since the Havanese produces small litters, breeders have great demand for their precious commodity. Beware of the shy or overly aggressive puppy: be especially conscious of the nervous Havanese pup. Don't let sentiment or emotion trap you into buying the runt of the litter.

Surely the colour of some Havanese in this book has attracted your eye. Many newcomers to the Havanese have strong prejudices toward one colour or another. In reality, colour in this breed has little bearing on the dog. The breed standard indicates no pref-

erence for colour, and that open-mindset should extend to pet selection as well. New owners should concern themselves with soundness of temperament and construction as well as freedom from congenital diseases. Although the

DID YOU KNOW?
Your puppy should have a well-fed appearance but not a distended abdomen, which may indicate worms or incorrect feeding, or both. The body should be firm, with a solid feel. The skin of the abdomen should be pale pink and clean, without signs of scratching or rash. Check the hind legs to make certain that dewclaws were removed, if any were present at birth.

51

black Havanese or the blonde Havanese captures your eye, for your heart's sake choose your puppy with your mind! Health, stable temperament, proper structure make for an ideal Havanese choice.

Breeders commonly allow visitors to see

DID YOU KNOW?

A good breeder should not be afraid to give you a health guarantee as well as a guarantee that the puppy will pass a temperment test administered by a vet or a trained dog behaviourist.

DID YOU KNOW?

Two important documents you will get from the breeder are the pup's pedigree and registration papers. The breeder should register the litter and each pup with The Kennel Club, and it is necessary for you to have the paperwork if you plan on showing or breeding in the future.

Make sure you know the breeder's intentions on which type of registration he will obtain for the pup. There are limited registrations which may prohibit the dog from being shown or from competing in non-conformation trials such as Working or Agility if the breeder feels that the pup is not of sufficient quality to do so. There is also a type of registration that will permit the dog in non-conformation competition only.

If your dog is registered with a Kennel-Club-recognised breed club, then you can register the pup with The Kennel Club yourself. Your breeder can assist you with the specifics of the registration process.

the litter by around the fifth or sixth week, and puppies leave for their new homes around the tenth week, rarely before. Breeders who permit their puppies to leave early are more interested in your pounds than their puppies' well being. Puppies need to learn the rules of the trade from their dams, and most dams continue teaching the pups manners, and dos and don'ts until around the eighth week. Breeders spend significant amounts of time with the Havanese toddlers so that they are able to interact with the 'other species', i.e., humans. Given the long history that dogs and humans have, bonding between the two species is natural but must be nurtured. A well-bred, well-socialised Bichon Havanese pup wants nothing more than to be near you and please you.

Always check the bite of your selected puppy to be sure that it is neither overshot or undershot. This may not be too noticeable on a young puppy but it is a fairly common problem with certain lines of Bichons Havaneses.

COMMITMENT OF OWNERSHIP

After considering all of these factors, you have most likely already made some very important decisions about selecting your puppy. You have chosen a Bichon Havanese, which means that you have decided which characteristics you want in a dog and what type of dog will best fit into your family and lifestyle. If you have selected a breeder, you have gone a step further—you have done your research and found a responsible, conscientious person who breeds quality Bichon Havanese and who should be a reliable source of help as you and your puppy adjust to life together. If you have observed a litter in action, you have obtained a first-hand look at the dynamics of a puppy 'pack' and, thus, you should learn about each pup's individual personality—perhaps you have even found one that particularly appeals to you.

However, even if you have not yet found the Bichon Havanese puppy of your dreams, observing pups will help you learn to recognise certain behaviour and to determine what a pup's behaviour indicates about his temperament. You will be able to pick out which pups are the leaders, which ones are less outgoing, which ones are confident, which ones are shy, playful, friendly, aggressive, etc. Equally as important, you will learn to

recognise what a healthy pup should look and act like. All of these things will help you in your search, and when you find the Bichon Havanese that was meant for you, you will know it!

Researching your breed, selecting a responsible breeder and observing as many pups as possible are all important steps on the way to dog ownership. It may seem like a lot of effort...and you have not even brought the pup home yet! Remember,

If you are interested in seeing Havaneses, attend a dog show to view the dogs in action, in this case, Ambar D' Sirius, a Cuban champion. It's a great place to meet breeders and owners and to make essential contacts. In Britain, the Havanese competes in the import registered classes.

DID YOU KNOW?

Breeders rarely release puppies until they are at least ten weeks of age. This is an acceptable age for most breeds of dog, excepting toy breeds which are not released until around 12 weeks, given their petite sizes. If a breeder has a puppy that is 12 weeks or more, it is likely well socialised and housetrained. Be sure that it is otherwise healthy before deciding to take it home.

53

Choose the puppy from the litter that exudes the most happiness and personality. This dam is Blanquita de la Giraldilla. Never take home the sad, timid puppy out of sympathy.

though, you cannot be too careful when it comes to deciding on the type of dog you want and finding out about your prospective pup's background. Buying a puppy is not—or should not be—just another whimsical purchase. This is one instance in which you actually do get to choose your own family! You may be thinking that buying a puppy should be fun—it should not be so serious and so much work. Keep in mind that your puppy is not a cuddly stuffed toy or decorative lawn ornament, but a creature that will become a real member of your family. You will come to realise that, whilst buying a puppy is a pleasurable and exciting endeavour, it is not something to be taken lightly. Relax…the fun will start when the pup comes home!

Always keep in mind that a puppy is nothing more than a baby in a furry disguise…a baby who is virtually helpless in a

DID YOU KNOW?

If you lead an erratic, unpredictable life, with daily or weekly changes in your work requirements, consider the problems of owning a puppy.

The new puppy has to be fed regularly, socialised (loved, petted, handled, introduced to other people) and, most importantly, allowed to visit outdoors for toilet training. As the dog gets older, it can be more tolerant of deviations in its feeding and toilet relief.

54

human world and who trusts his owner for fulfilment of his basic needs for survival. In addition to water and shelter, your pup needs care, protection, guidance and love. If you are not prepared to commit to this, then you are not prepared to own a dog.

Wait a minute, you say. How hard could this be? All of my neighbours own dogs and they seem to be doing just fine. Why should I have to worry about all of this? Well, you should not worry about it; in fact, you will probably find that once your Bichon Havanese pup gets used to his new home, he will fall into his place in the family quite naturally. But it never hurts to emphasise the commitment of dog ownership. With some time

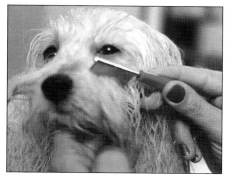

Whilst the Havanese appears to be an easycare, no-maintenance dog, its hallmark silky coat requires some time and energy from its owner.

and patience, it is really not too difficult to raise a curious and exuberant Bichon Havanese pup to be a well-adjusted and well-mannered adult dog—a dog that could be your most loyal friend.

PREPARING PUPPY'S PLACE IN YOUR HOME

Researching your breed and finding a breeder are only two aspects of the 'homework' you will have to do before bringing your Bichon Havanese puppy home. You will also have to prepare your home and family for the new addition. Much as you would

Are you willing to devote the proper time to keep your Havanese looking his absolute best?

DID YOU KNOW?
If the breeder from whom you are buying a puppy asks you a lot of personal questions, do not be insulted. Such a breeder wants to be sure that you will be a fit provider for his puppy.

55

prepare a nursery for a new-born baby, you will need to designate a place in your home that will be the puppy's own. How you prepare your home will depend on how much freedom the dog will be allowed. Whatever you decide, you must ensure that he has a place that he can 'call his own.'

When you bring your new puppy into your home, you are bringing him into what will become his home as well. Obviously, you did not buy a puppy so that he could take over your house, but in order for a puppy to grow into a stable, well-adjusted dog, he has to feel comfortable in his surroundings. Remember, he is leaving the warmth and security of his mother and litter-mates, as well as the familiarity of the only place he has ever known, so it is important to make his transition as easy as possible. By preparing a

DID YOU KNOW?

The cost of food must also be mentioned. All dogs need a good quality food with an adequate supply of protein to develop their bones and muscles properly. Most dogs are not picky eaters but unless fed properly they can quickly succumb to skin problems.

DID YOU KNOW?

During crate training, you should partition off the section of the crate in which the pup stays. If he is given too big an area, this will hinder your training efforts. Crate training is based on the fact that a dog does not like to soil his sleeping quarters, so it is ineffective to keep a pup in a crate that is so big that he can eliminate in one end and get far enough away from it to sleep. Also, you want to make the crate den-like for the pup. Blankets and a favourite toy will make the crate cosy for the small pup; as he grows, you may want to evict some of his 'roommates' to make more room.

It will take some coaxing at first, but be patient. Given some time to get used to it, your pup will adapt to his new home-within-a-home quite nicely.

place in your home for the puppy, you are making him feel as welcome as possible in a strange new place. It should not take him long to get used to it, but the sudden shock of being transplanted is somewhat traumatic for a young pup. Imagine how a small child would feel in the same situation—that is how your puppy must be feeling. It is up to you to reassure him and to let him know, 'Little fellow, you are going to like it here!'

WHAT YOU SHOULD BUY
CRATE

To someone unfamiliar with the use of crates in dog training, it may seem like punishment to shut a dog in a crate, but this is at least debatable. Although all breeders do not advocate crate training, more and more breeders and trainers are recommending crates as a preferred tool for pet puppies as well as show puppies. They argue that crates are not cruel—and have many humane and highly effective uses in dog care and training. For example, crate training is a very popular and very successful housebreaking method. A crate can keep your dog safe during travel; and, perhaps most importantly, a crate provides your dog with a place of his own in your home. It serves as a 'doggie bedroom' of sorts—your Bichon Havanese can curl up in his crate when he wants to sleep or when he just needs a break. Many dogs sleep in their crates overnight. When lined with soft bed-

PHOTO COURTESY OF MIKKI PET PRODUCTS.

Crates can be purchased at your local pet shop. Crate training is amongst the newest innovations in dog care. Top breeders around the world are convinced that crate training is the best way to housebreak and train a dog. Your pet shop will offer a variety of sizes, styles and colours.

ding and filled with his favourite toys, a crate becomes a cosy pseudo-den for your dog. Like his ancestors, he too will seek out the comfort and retreat of a den—especially if the door is left open so he can go in and out of his own accord.

As far as purchasing a crate, the type that you buy is up to you. It will most likely be one of the two most popular types: wire or fibreglass. There are advantages and disadvantages to each

DID YOU KNOW?

Do not keep an adult dog in a crate for more than two hours at a time. If you keep him crated during the day while you are working, he'll develop into a day-sleeper and a night marauder.

type. For example, a wire crate is more open, allowing the air to flow through and affording the dog a view of what is going on around him whilst a fibreglass crate is sturdier. Both can double as travel crates, providing protection for the dog. A medium-size crate is the best choice for the Havanese, who will stand approximately 21 inches at his mature height.

BEDDING

Veterinary bedding in the dog's crate will help the dog feel more at home and you may also like to pop in a small blanket. This will take the place of the leaves, twigs, etc., that the pup would

Special delivery! A Havanese puppy is not a toy. New owners must be prepared to accommodate the young pup with everything it needs to live.

use in the wild to make a den; the pup can make his own 'burrow' in the crate. Although your pup is far removed from his den-making ancestors, the denning instinct is still a part of his genetic makeup. Second, until you bring your pup home, he has been sleeping amidst the warmth of his mother and littermates, and whilst a blanket is not the same as a warm, breathing body, it still provides heat and something with which to snuggle. You will want to wash your pup's bedding frequently in case he has an accident in his crate, and replace or remove any blanket that becomes ragged and starts to fall apart.

TOYS

Toys are a must for dogs of all ages, especially for curious playful pups. Puppies are the 'children' of the dog world, and what child does not love toys? Chew toys provide enjoyment to both

(FACING PAGE) Provide your Havanese with an appropriately sized crate. In no time, your Havanese will accept his crate as his own den, a place to which he can retire and spend some time by himself.

Your pet shop will carry many essential items for your Havanese, including toys, grooming supplies, crates, bowls and more. Dog ownership is an expensive proposition. Can you provide a proper home for a Havanese?

59

By nature, the Havanese, like most other dogs, is playful and animated. You should purchase appropriate toys for your Havanese that are safe and chew-worthy. This is Caramba Coquito, owned by Zoila Portuondo.

dog and owner—your dog will enjoy playing with his favourite toys, whilst you will enjoy the fact that they distract him from your expensive shoes and leather sofa. Puppies love to chew; in fact, chewing is a physical need for pups as they are teething, and everything looks appetising! The full range of your possessions—from old dishcloth to Oriental rug—are fair game in the eyes of a teething pup. Puppies are not all that discerning when it comes to finding something to literally 'sink their teeth into'—everything tastes great!

Breeders advise owners to resist stuffed toys, because they can become de-stuffed in no time. The overly excited pup may ingest the stuffing, which is neither digestible nor nutritious. Similarly, squeaky toys are quite popular, but should be avoided

Your Havanese puppy will appreciate soft bedding for his sleeping area. Be certain that your puppy does not have access to toys that are too small that can be accidentally swallowed. Supervision is advisable whenever puppies are playing with rubber toys.

PHOTO COURTESY OF MIKKI PET PRODUCTS.

Pet shops offer a wide selection of suitable dog toys that your Havanese will welcome. Never offer your dog toys that are manufactured for children as they may be dangerous to a teething puppy.

for the Bichon Havanese. Perhaps a squeaky toy can be used as an aid in training, but not for free play. If a pup 'disembowels' one of these, the small plastic squeaker inside can be dangerous if swallowed. Monitor the condition of all your pup's toys carefully and get rid of any that have been chewed to the point of becoming potentially dangerous.

Be careful of natural bones, which have a tendency to splinter into sharp, dangerous pieces. Also be careful of rawhide, which can turn into pieces that are easy to swallow or into a mushy mess on your carpet.

DID YOU KNOW?

With a big variety of dog toys available, and so many that look like they would be a lot of fun for a dog, be careful in your selection. It is amazing what a set of puppy teeth can do to an innocent-looking toy, so, obviously, safety is a major consideration. Be sure to choose the most durable products that you can find. Hard nylon bones and toys are a safe bet, and many of them are offered in different scents and flavours that will be sure to capture your dog's attention. It is always fun to play a game of catch with your dog, and there are balls and flying discs that are specially made to withstand dog teeth.

Lead

A nylon lead is probably the best option as it is the most resistant to puppy teeth should your pup take a liking to chewing on his lead. Of course, this is a habit that should be nipped in the bud, but if your pup likes to chew on his lead he has a very slim chance of being able to chew through the strong nylon. Nylon leads are also lightweight, which is good for a young Bichon Havanese who is just getting used to the idea of walking on a lead. For everyday walking and safety purposes, the nylon lead is a good choice. As your pup grows up and gets used to walking on the lead, you may want to purchase a flexible lead. These leads allow you to extend the length to give the dog a broader area to explore or to shorten the length to keep the close to you.

Collar

Your pup should get used to wearing a collar outside the house since you will want to attach his ID tags to it. You have to attach the lead to something! A lightweight nylon collar is a good choice; make sure that it fits snugly enough so that the pup cannot wriggle out of it, but is loose enough so that it will not be uncomfortably tight around the pup's neck. You should be able to fit a finger between the pup and the collar. When your Havanese is at home, consider removing the collar as it can ruin the coat.

Food and Water Bowls

Your pup will need two bowls, one for food and one for water. You may want two sets of bowls, one for inside and one for outside, depending on where the dog will be fed and where he will be spending most of his time. Stainless steel or sturdy plastic bowls are popular choices. Plastic bowls are more chewable. Dogs tend not to chew on the steel variety, which can be sterilised. It is important to buy sturdy bowls since anything is in danger of being chewed by puppy teeth and you do not

Most trainers recommend using a lightweight nylon lead for your Havanese. Pet shops offer dozens of choices for collars and leads, in different styles, colours and lengths.

Choose the Right Collar

The BUCKLE or LEATHER COLLAR is the standard collar used for walking your dog. Be sure that you adjust the buckle on growing puppies. Check it every day. It can become too tight overnight! These collars can be made of leather or nylon. Attach your dog's identification tags to this collar.

The CHOKE CHAIN is the usual collar recommended for training. It is constructed of highly polished steel so that it slides easily through the stainless steel loop. The idea is that the dog controls the pressure around its neck and he will stop pulling if the collar becomes uncomfortable. Never leave a choke collar on your dog when not training.

The HALTER is for a trained dog that has to be restrained to prevent running away, chasing a cat and the like. Considered the most humane of all collars, it is frequently used on smaller dogs for which collars are not comfortable. The halter is removed when the dog is in the home.

The SELF-CORRECTING COLLAR certainly appears ominous, like an ancient instrument of torture. Although it is not intended to 'torture' a dog, it is only recommended on the most difficult of dogs, and never on small dogs. It should only be employed by someone who knows how to use it properly.

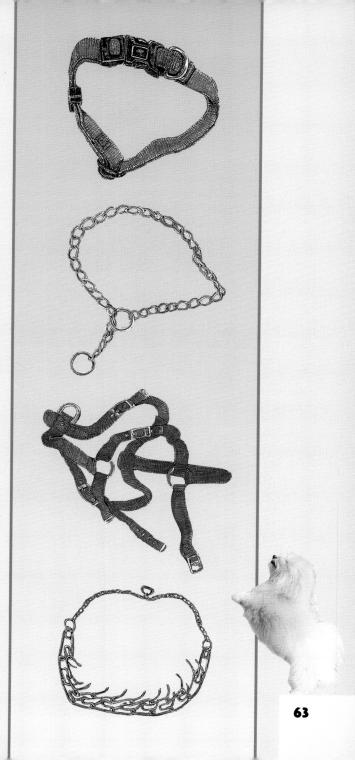

Provide .your Havanese with feeding and watering bowls. These bowls can be constructed of sturdy plastic, ceramic, clay or stainless steel. The stainless steel ones are most dependable, durable and sanitary.

want your dog to be constantly chewing apart his bowl (for his safety and for your purse!).

CLEANING SUPPLIES

Until a pup is housetrained you will be doing a lot of cleaning. Accidents will occur, which is okay in the beginning because the puppy does not know any

better. All you can do is be prepared to clean up any 'accidents.' Old rags, towels, newspapers and a safe disinfectant are good to have on hand.

BEYOND THE BASICS

The items previously discussed are the bare necessities. You will find out what else you need as you go along—grooming supplies, flea/tick protection, baby gates to partition a room, etc. These things will vary depending on your situation but it is important that you have everything you need to feed and make your Bichon Havanese comfortable in his first few days at home.

PHOTO COURTESY OF MIKKI PET PRODUCTS.

PUPPY-PROOFING YOUR HOME

Aside from making sure that your Bichon Havanese will be comfortable in your home, you also have to make sure that your home is safe for your Bichon Havanese.

This means taking precautions that your pup will not get into anything he should not get into and that there is nothing within his reach that may harm him should he sniff it, chew it, inspect it, etc. This probably seems obvious since, whilst you are primarily concerned with your pup's safety, at the same time you do not want your belongings to be ruined. Breakables should be placed out of reach of the area designated for your dog. This area should also be free of any potentially dangerous items. An electrical cord can pose a danger should the puppy decide to taste it—and who is going to convince a pup that it would not make a great chew toy? Cords should be fastened tightly against the wall. If your dog is going to spend time in a crate, make sure that there is nothing near his crate that he can reach if he sticks his curious little nose or paws through the openings. Just as you would with a child, keep all household cleaners and chemicals where the pup cannot get to them.

It is also important to make sure that the outside of your home is safe. Of course your puppy should never be unsupervised, but a pup let loose in the garden will want to run and explore, and he should be granted that freedom. Do not let a fence give you a false sense of security; you would be surprised how crafty (and persistent) a dog can be in figuring out how to dig under and squeeze his way through small holes, or to jump or climb over a fence. The remedy is to make the fence high enough so that it really is impossible for your dog to get over it (about 3 metres should suffice), and well embedded into the ground. Be sure to repair or secure any gaps in the fence. Check the fence periodically to ensure

Responsible, law-abiding dog owners pick up their dogs' dropping whenever they are in public. Pooper-scooper devices make the job quick and easy.

that it is in good shape and make repairs as needed; a very determined pup may return to the same spot to 'work on it' until he is able to get through.

FIRST TRIP TO THE VET

You have picked out your puppy, and your home and family are ready. Now all you have to do is collect your Bichon Havanese from the breeder and the fun begins, right? Well...not so fast. Something else you need to prepare is your pup's first trip to the veterinary surgeon. You should have an appointment arranged for your pup before you pick him up and plan on taking him for an examination before bringing him home.

Puppies are naturally curious and will attempt to chew on anything they find. Owners should keep all destructible, valuable items away from the exploring Havanese pup.

DID YOU KNOW?

Thoroughly puppy-proof your house before your puppy comes home. Never use roach or rodent poisons in any area accessible to the puppy. Avoid the use of toilet bowl cleaners. Most dogs are born with toilet bowl sonar and will take a drink if the lid is left open. Also keep the trash secured and out of reach.

The pup's first visit will consist of an overall examination to make sure that the pup does not have any problems that are not apparent to the eye. The veterinary surgeon will also set up a schedule for the pup's vaccinations; the breeder will inform you of which ones the pup has already received and the vet can continue from there.

INTRODUCTION TO THE FAMILY

Everyone in the house will be excited about the puppy coming home and will want to pet him and play with him, but it is best to make the introduction low-key so as not to overwhelm the puppy. He is apprehensive already. It is the first time he has been separated from his mother and the breeder, and the ride to your home is likely the first time he has been in an auto. The last thing you want to do is smother him, as this will only frighten him further. This is not to say that human contact is not extremely necessary at this stage, because this is the time when a connection between the pup and his human family is formed. Gentle petting and soothing words should help console him, as well as just putting him down and letting him explore on his own (under your watchful eye, of course).

The pup may approach the family members or may busy himself with exploring for a while. Gradually, each person should spend some time with the pup, one at a time, crouching down to get as close to the pup's level as possible and letting him sniff their hands and petting him gently. He definitely needs human attention and he needs to be touched—this is how to form an immediate bond. Just remember that the pup is experiencing a lot of things for the first time, at the same time. There are new people, new noises, new smells, and new things to investigate: so be gentle, be affectionate, and be as comforting as you can be.

YOUR PUP'S FIRST NIGHT HOME

You have travelled home with your new charge safely in his basket or crate. He's been to the vet for a thorough check-over; he's been weighed, his papers examined; perhaps he's even been vaccinated

and wormed as well. He's met the family, licked the whole family, including the excited children and the less-than-happy cat. He's explored his area, his new bed, the garden and anywhere else he's been permitted. He's eaten his first meal at home and

DID YOU KNOW?
Taking your dog from the breeder to your home in a car can be a very uncomfortable experience for both of you. The puppy will have been taken from his warm, friendly, safe environment and brought into a strange new environment. An environment that moves! Be prepared for loose bowels, urination, crying, whining and even fear biting. With proper love and encouragement when you arrive home, the stress of the trip should quickly disappear.

DID YOU KNOW?
It will take at least two weeks for your puppy to become accustomed to his new surroundings. Give him lots of love, attention, handling, frequent opportunities to relieve himself, a diet he likes to eat and a place he can call his own.

Your Havanese family is growing and growing! Even experienced owners can find the first night with a new Havanese puppy stressful. Mother, daughter and granddaughter: Dolly, Epoca and Blanquita de la Giraldilla, with a pup from Blanquita's litter.

68

relieved himself in the proper place. He's heard lots of new sounds, smelled new friends and seen more of the outside world than ever before.

That was just the first day! He's worn out and is ready for bed...or so you think!

It's puppy's first night and you are ready to say 'Good night'—keep in mind that this is puppy's first night ever to be sleeping alone. His dam and littermates are no longer at paw's length and he's a bit scared, cold and lonely. Be reassuring to your new family member. This is not the time to spoil him and give in to his inevitable whining.

Puppies whine. They whine to let the others know where they are and hopefully to get company out of it. Place your pup in his new bed or crate in his room and close the door. Mercifully, he may fall asleep without a peep. If the inevitable

occurs, ignore the whining: he is fine. Be strong and keep his interest in mind. Do not allow your heart to become guilty and visit the pup. He will fall asleep.

Many breeders recommend placing a piece of bedding from his former homestead in his new bed so that he recognises the scent of his littermates. Others still advise placing a hot water bottle in his bed for warmth. This latter may be a good idea provided the pup doesn't attempt to suckle—he'll get good and wet and may not fall asleep so fast.

Puppy's first night can be somewhat stressful for the pup and his new family. Remember that you are setting the tone of nighttime at your house. . Unless you want to play with your pup every evening at 10 p.m., midnight and 2 a.m., don't initiate the habit. Your family will thank you, and so will your pup!

A basket with veterinary bedding is an excellent choice for the new puppy. Offer the puppy a safe chew toy to take to his new bed.

PREVENTING PUPPY PROBLEMS

SOCIALISATION

Now that you have done all of the preparatory work and have helped your pup get accustomed to his new home and family, it is about time for you to have some fun! Socialising your Bichon Havanese pup gives

you the opportunity to show off your new friend, and your pup gets to reap the benefits of being an adorable furry creature that people will want to pet and, in general, think is absolutely precious!

Besides getting to know his new family, your puppy should be exposed to other people, animals and situations, but of course he must not come into close contact with dogs you don't know well until his course of injections is fully complete. This will help him become well adjusted as he grows up and less prone to being timid or fearful of the new things he will encounter. Your pup's socialisation began at the breeder's but now it is your responsibility to continue it. The socialisation he receives up until the age of 12 weeks is the most critical, as this is the time when he forms his impressions of the outside world. Be especially careful during the eight-to-ten-week period, also known as the fear period. The interaction he receives during this time should be gentle and reassuring. Lack of socialisation can manifest itself in fear and aggression as the dog grows up. He needs lots of human contact, affection, handling and exposure to other animals.

Once your pup has received his necessary vaccinations, feel free to take him out and about (on his lead, of course). Walk him around the

DID YOU KNOW?

An important consideration to be discussed is the sex of your puppy. For a family companion, a bitch may be the better choice, considering the female's inbred concern for all young creatures and her accompanying tolerance and patience. It is always advised to spay a pet bitch, which may guarantee her a longer life.

neighbourhood, take him on your daily errands, let people pet him, let him meet other dogs and pets, etc. Puppies do not have to try to make friends; there will be no shortage of people who will want to introduce themselves. Just make sure that you carefully supervise each meeting. If the neighbourhood children want to say hello, for example, that is great—children and pups most

Havaneses destined for the show ring require extensive dog-to-dog socialisation. Show dogs encounter each other regularly. Your Havanese must accept other dogs without reservations. This dog show is underway in Havana.

DID YOU KNOW?

Training your puppy takes much patience and can be frustrating at times, but you should see results from your efforts. If you have a puppy that seems untrainable, take him to a trainer or behaviourist. The dog may have a personality problem that requires the help of a professional, or perhaps you need help in learning how to train your dog.

often make great companions. Sometimes an excited child can unintentionally handle a pup too roughly, or an overzealous pup can playfully nip a little too hard. You want to make socialisation experiences positive ones. What a pup learns during this very formative stage will impact his attitude toward future encounters. You want your dog to be comfortable around everyone. A pup that has a bad experience with a child may grow up to be a dog that is shy around or aggressive toward children.

CONSISTENCY IN TRAINING

Dogs, being pack animals, naturally need a leader, or else they try to establish dominance in their packs. When you bring a dog into your family, the choice of who becomes the leader and who becomes the 'pack' is entirely up to you! Your pup's intuitive quest for dominance, coupled with the fact that it is nearly impossible to look at an

DID YOU KNOW?

Thorough socialisation includes not only meeting new people but also being introduced to new experiences such as riding in the auto, having his coat brushed, hearing the television, walking in a crowd—the list is endless. The more your pup experiences, and the more positive the experiences are, the less of a shock and the less scary it will be for your pup to encounter new things.

adorable Bichon Havanese pup, with his 'puppy-dog' eyes and fuzzy charms, and not cave in, give the pup almost an unfair advantage in getting the upper hand! A pup will definitely test the waters to see what he can and cannot do. Do not give in to those pleading eyes— stand your ground when it comes to disciplining the pup and make sure that all family members do the same. It will only confuse the pup when Mother tells him to get off the couch when he is used to sitting up there with Father to watch the nightly news. Avoid discrepancies by having all members of the household decide on the rules before the pup even comes home…and be consistent in enforcing them! Early training shapes the dog's personality, so you cannot be unclear in what you expect.

COMMON PUPPY PROBLEMS

The best way to prevent puppy problems is to be proactive in stopping an undesirable behaviour as soon as it starts. The old saying 'You can't teach an old dog new tricks' does not necessarily hold true, but it is true that it is much easier to discourage bad behaviour in a

young developing pup than to wait until the pup's bad behaviour becomes the adult dog's bad habit. There are some problems that are especially prevalent in puppies as they develop.

NIPPING

As puppies start to teethe, they feel the need to sink their teeth into anything available…unfortunately that includes your fingers, arms, hair, and toes. You may find this behaviour cute for the first five seconds…until you feel just how sharp those puppy teeth are. This is something you want to discourage immediately and consistently with a firm 'No!' Then replace your finger with an appropriate chew toy. Whilst this behaviour is merely annoying when the dog is young, it can become dangerous as your adult Havanese thinks it is acceptable to nibble on human appendages.

CRYING

Your pup will often cry, whine, whimper, howl or make some type of commotion when he is left alone. This is basically his way of calling out for attention to make sure that you know he is there and that you have not forgotten about him. He

It is essential for new owners to meet the dam as well as the litter when visiting the breeder. The dam's temperament and behaviour will indicate much about her progeny.

feels insecure when he is left alone, when you are out of the house and he is in his crate or when you are in another part of the house and he cannot see you. The noise he is making is an expression of the anxiety he feels at being alone, so he needs to be taught that being alone is OK. You are not actually training the dog to stop making noise, you are training him to feel comfortable when he is alone and thus removing the need for him to make the noise. This is where the crate filled with cosy bedding and toys comes in handy. You want to know that he is safe when you are not there to supervise, and you know that he will be safe in his crate rather than roaming freely about the house. In order for the pup to stay in his crate without making a fuss, he needs to be comfortable in his crate. At the same time, he should not be confined too long in his crate and his area in the house should be expanded as he grows. It is extremely important that the crate is never used as a form of punishment, or the pup will have a negative association with the crate.

Accustom the pup to the crate in short, gradually increasing time intervals in which you put him in the crate or in a larger pen, maybe with a treat, and stay in the room with him. If he cries or makes a fuss, do not go to him, but stay in his sight. Gradually he will realise that staying alone is all right, and it will not be so traumatic for him when

you are not around. You may want to leave the radio on softly when you leave the house; the sound of human voices may be comforting to him.

DID YOU KNOW?
Chewing goes hand in hand with nipping in the sense that a teething puppy is always looking for a way to soothe his aching gums. In this case, instead of chewing on you, he may have taken a liking to your favourite shoe or something else which he should not be chewing. Again, realise that this is a normal canine behaviour that does not need to be discouraged, only redirected. Your pup just needs to be taught what is acceptable to chew on and what is off limits. Consistently tell him NO when you catch him chewing on something forbidden and give him a chew toy. Conversely, praise him when you catch him chewing on something appropriate. In this way you are discouraging the inappropriate behaviour and reinforcing the desired behaviour. The puppy chewing should stop after his adult teeth have come in, but an adult dog continues to chew for various reasons—perhaps because he is bored, perhaps to relieve tension, or perhaps he just likes to chew. That is why it is important to redirect his chewing when he is still young.

FEEDING CONSIDERATIONS

Originally, the dog was a carnivorous animal, but centuries of domesticity and human company have changed him into an omnivore, which is a good thing.

DID YOU KNOW?

Selecting the best dry dog food is difficult. There is no majority consensus among veterinary scientists as to the value of nutrient analyses (protein, fat, fibre, moisture, ash, cholesterol, minerals, etc.). All agree that feeding trials are what matters, but you also have to consider the individual dog. Its weight, age, activity and what pleases its taste, all must be considered. It is probably best to take the advice of your veterinary surgeon. Every dog's dietary requirements vary, even during the lifetime of a particular dog.

If your dog is fed a good dry food, it does not require supplements of meat or vegetables. Dogs do appreciate a little variety in their diets so you may choose to stay with the same brand, but vary the flavour. Alternatively you may wish to add a little flavoured stock to give a difference to the taste.

So, along with a portion of meat and proteins of animal origin, vegetables and fruits can be added to his diet to keep him healthy. Avoid sweets and fried foods and, of course, never give your dog small bones. Many commercial dried dog foods contain all the proteins and minerals your dog needs for a complete and healthy diet.

Today the choices of food for your Bichon Havanese are many and varied. There are simply dozens of brands of food in all sorts of flavours and textures, ranging from puppy diets to those for seniors. There are even hypoallergenic and low-calorie diets available. Because your Bichon Havanese's food has a bearing on coat, health and temperament, it is essential that the most suitable diet is selected for a Bichon Havanese of his age. It is fair to say, however, that even dedicated owners can be somewhat perplexed by the enormous range of foods available. Only understanding what is best for your dog will help you reach a valued decision.

Dog foods are produced in three basic types: dried, semi-

DID YOU KNOW?

You must store your dry dog food carefully. Open packages of dog food quickly lose their vitamin value, usually within 90 days of being opened. Mould spores and vermin could also contaminate the food.

Given the advances of dog food companies today, feeding your Havanese can be fairly simple. Your breeder and vet can recommend a reliable brand of dog food on which to start your puppy.

moist and tinned. Dried foods are useful for the cost-conscious for overall they tend to be less expensive than semi-moist or tinned. These contain the least fat and the most preservatives. In general tinned foods are made up of 60—70 percent water, whilst semi-moist ones often contain so much sugar that they are perhaps the least preferred by owners, even though their dogs seem to like them.

When selecting your dog's diet, three stages of development must be considered: the puppy stage, adult stage and the senior or veteran stage.

PUPPY STAGE

Puppies instinctively want to suck milk from their mother's teats and a normal puppy will exhibit this behaviour from just a few moments following birth. If puppies do not attempt to suckle within the first half-hour or so, they should be encouraged to do so by placing them on a nipple, having

selected ones with plenty of milk. This early milk supply is important in providing colostrum to protect the puppies during the first eight to ten weeks of their lives. Although a mother's milk is

DID YOU KNOW?

A good test for proper diet is the colour, odour, and firmness of your dog's stool. A healthy dog usually produces three semi-hard stools per day. The stools should have no unpleasant odour. They should be the same colour from excretion to excretion.

Puppies nurse from the dam for the first six weeks. Weaning begins around the third or fourth week by introducing cereals and solid foods.

DID YOU KNOW?

Dog food must be at room temperature, neither too hot nor too cold. Fresh water, changed daily and served in a clean bowl, is mandatory, especially when feeding dry food.

Never feed your dog from the table while you are eating. Never feed your dog left-overs from your own meal. They usually contain too much fat and too much seasoning.

Dogs must chew their food. Hard pellets are excellent; soups and slurries are to be avoided.

Don't add left-overs or any extras to normal dog food. The normal food is usually balanced and adding something extra destroys the balance.

Except for age-related changes, dogs do not require dietary variations. They can be fed the same diet, day after day, without their becoming bored or ill.

much better than any milk formula, despite there being some excellent ones available, if the puppies do not feed you will have to feed them yourself. For those with less experience, advice from a veterinary surgeon is important so that you feed not only the right quantity of milk but that of correct quality, fed at suitably frequent intervals, usually every two hours during the first few days of life.

Puppies should be allowed to nurse from their mothers for about the first six weeks, although from the third or fourth week you will have begun to introduce small portions of suitable solid food. Most breeders like to introduce alternate milk and meat meals initially, building up to weaning time.

By the time the puppies are seven or a maximum of eight weeks old, they should be fully weaned and fed solely on a proprietary puppy food. Selection of the most suitable, good-quality diet at this time is essential for a puppy's fastest growth rate is during the first year of life. Veterinary surgeons are usually able to offer advice in this regard and, although the frequency of meals will have been reduced over time, only when a young dog has reached the age of about 18 months should an adult diet be fed.

Puppy and junior diets should be well balanced for the needs of your dog, so that except in certain circumstances additional vitamins, minerals and proteins will not be required.

ADULT DIETS

A dog is considered an adult when it has stopped growing, so in general the diet of a Bichon Havanese can be changed to an adult one at about 10 to 12 months of age. Again you should rely upon your veterinary surgeon or dietary specialist to recommend an acceptable maintenance diet. Major dog food manufacturers specialise in this type of food, and it is just necessary for you to select the one best suited to your dog's needs. Active dogs may have different requirements than sedate dogs.

DID YOU KNOW?
Many adult diets are based on grain. There is nothing wrong with this as long as it does not contain soy meal. Diets based on soy often cause flatulence (passing gas).

Grain-based diets are almost always the least expensive and a good grain diet is just as good as the most expensive diet containing animal protein.

There are many cases, however, when your dog might require a special diet. These special requirements should only be recommended by your veterinary surgeon.

Adult dogs may only require one feeding a day, though some breeders recommend offering two smaller meals.

77

Senior Diets

As dogs get older, their metabolism changes. The older dog usually exercises less, moves more slowly and sleeps more. This change in lifestyle and physiological performance requires a change in diet. Since these changes take place slowly, they might not be recognisable. What is easily recognisable is weight gain. By continuing to feed your dog an adult-maintenance diet when it is slowing down metabolically, your dog will gain weight. Obesity in an older dog compounds the health problems that already accompany old age.

As your dog gets older, few of their organs function up to par. The kidneys slow down and the intestines become less efficient. These age-related factors are best handled with a change in diet and a change in feeding schedule to give smaller portions that are more easily digested.

There is no single best diet for every older dog. Whilst many dogs do well on light or senior diets, other dogs do better on puppy diets or other special premium diets such as lamb and rice. Be sensitive to your senior Bichon Havanese's diet and this will help control other problems that may arise with your old friend.

Although the Havanese is a small dog, he enjoys the opportunity to stretch his legs. It is not wise to allow your Havanese to run off-lead near a roadway.

Water

Just as your dog needs proper nutrition from his food, water is an essential "nutrient" as well. Water keeps the dog's body properly hydrated and promotes normal function of the body's systems. During housebreaking it is necessary to keep an eye on how much water your Bichon Havanese is drinking, but once he is reliably trained he should have access to clean fresh water at all times. Make sure that the dog's water bowl is clean, and change the water often, making sure that water is always available for your dog, especially if you feed dried food.

Exercise

Although a Bichon Havanese is small, all dogs require some form of exercise, regardless of size. A sedentary lifestyle is as harmful to a dog as it is to a person. The Bichon Havanese is a fairly active breed that enjoys exercise, but you don't have to be an Olympic athlete! Regular walks, play sessions in the garden, or letting the dog run free

What are you feeding your dog?

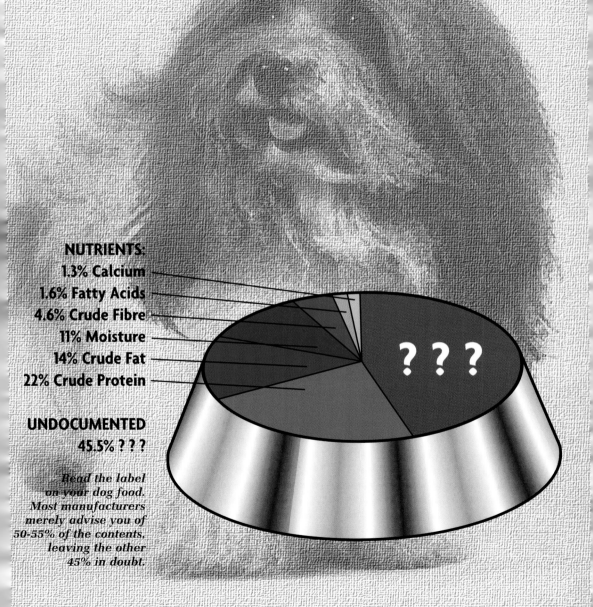

NUTRIENTS:
1.3% Calcium
1.6% Fatty Acids
4.6% Crude Fibre
11% Moisture
14% Crude Fat
22% Crude Protein

UNDOCUMENTED
45.5% ? ? ?

Read the label on your dog food. Most manufacturers merely advise you of 50-55% of the contents, leaving the other 45% in doubt.

???

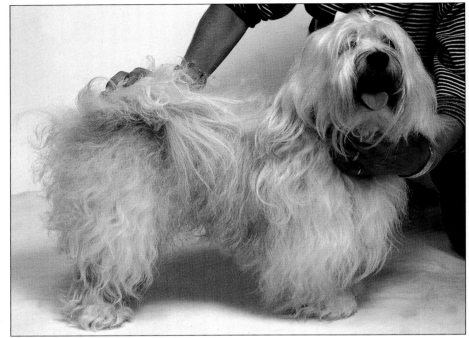

Maintaining the long, silky coat of the Havanese is not as difficult as it looks and the coat doesn't shed.

(FACING PAGE) Normal dog hairs enlarged 200 times original size. Inset shows the tip of a growing hair enlarged 1000 times. Scanning electron micrograph (S.E.M.) by Dr. Dennis Kunkel, University of Hawaii.

DID YOU KNOW?

How much grooming equipment you purchase will depend on how much grooming you are going to do. Here are some basics:

- Natural bristle brush
- Slicker brush
- Metal comb
- Scissors
- Blaster
- Rubber mat
- Dog shampoo
- Spray hose attachment
- Ear cleaner
- Cotton buds
- Towels
- Nail clippers

in the garden under your supervision are sufficient forms of exercise for the Havanese. For those who are more ambitious, you will find that your Bichon Havanese also enjoys long walks, an occasional hike or even a swim! Bear in mind that an overweight dog should never be over-exercised suddenly; instead he should be allowed to increase exercise slowly. Not only is exercise essential to keep the dog's body fit, it is essential to his mental well being. A bored dog will find something to do, which often manifests itself in some

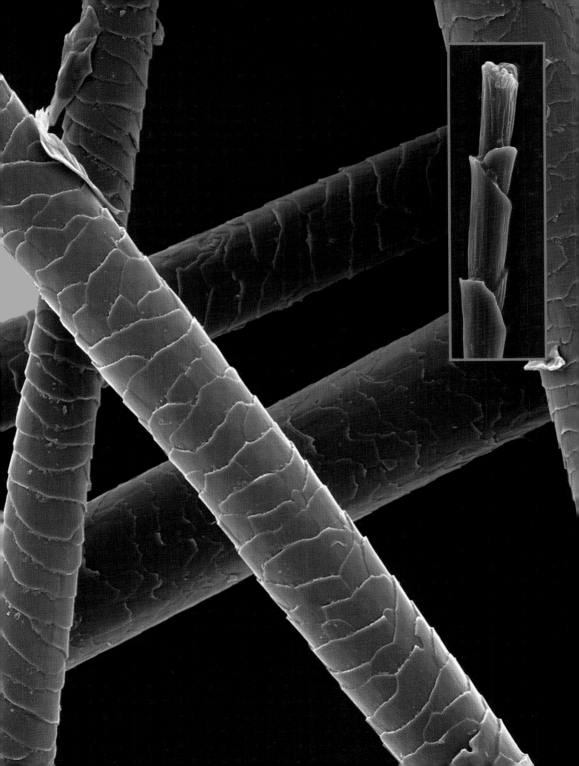

type of destructive behaviour. In this sense, it is essential for the owner's mental well being as well!

GROOMING

BRUSHING

Professional groomers will place the Havanese on a table, leashed for safety, and brush the coat as they fluff it with an electric dryer. The novice may prefer to use the blaster first and brush the coat once it is dry.

If we use the first method, we should use a brush or soft rake. With the second method, we need a metal comb with separated teeth (about eight teeth per inch). In both cases we should be aware that our dog has to be groomed by layers. That means that the different layers of

Your local pet shop will have a large supply of grooming tools that you can use on your Havanese.

Do not divide the Havanese's coat in half when combing it. Groom one area at a time, beginning with the comb to ensure that there are no tangles. Then brush over the area.

A small metal comb is useful on the Havanese's muzzle.

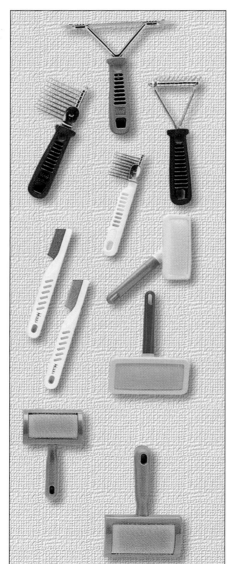

PHOTO COURTESY OF MIKKI PET PRODUCTS.

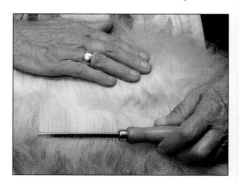

Once the ears have been combed, gently brush over them to give them a natural look.

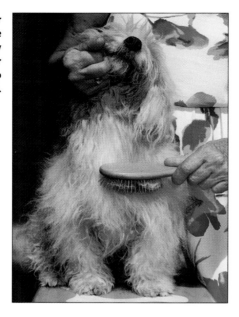

Brush the layer closest to the skin first, slowly working your way to the top layer.

The beauty of a well-groomed Havanese is that she still looks tousled and carefree! This is Bella, owned by Katy Trevilla of Cuba. The dog should never have the clipped, well-coiffed appearance of a Bichon Frise or Poodle.

the coat are raised and groomed separately, beginning with the layer closest to the skin and ending with the top or outer layer, which is what we see. Begin with legs and feet, continue with tail and trunk, working from back to front, then do the chest and neck and, finally, the head. In the nozzle zone, it is preferable to use a smaller metal comb with closer teeth.

You can avoid matting by using this method to groom your dry dog at least twice a week. When you're combing, be careful not to pull out the hair. It's best to work a small area at a time, slowly and patiently, to prevent the undesirable loss of hair. If you occasionally run into a mat-

ted layer, we recommend the following treatment.

Avoid cutting the knots. Try to untangle each one with your fingers, pulling the hairs from the centre outward. Once the knot is opened with the fingers, you can use a mat and tangle comb. This is a special comb that has long, well-spaced teeth with rounded ends to prevent skin injury. In using it, you should always hold the tuft of hair between your fingers close to the skin, so the dog won't be hurt. Also take care to prevent the unnecessary elimination of tufts.

Groom your Havanese by area, but don't divide the coat in half, as some people do, by creating a part that runs the full length of the back and even up

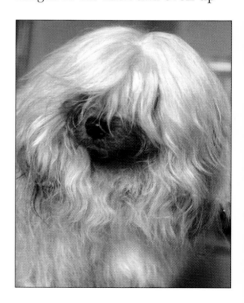

the neck and head. This distorts the image of the dog. Rather, once you've combed an area and are certain the entire layer is untangled, brush the layer lightly and let it fall. The Havanese will shake itself and the hair will fall naturally where it belongs.

BATHING

Generally speaking, dogs should be bathed before being groomed. The Havanese that lives in a tropical climate needs to be bathed monthly if its coat is dirty, but one way to keep the dog's coat clean is to give it dry baths with talcum powder. In a cold climate, the Havanese should be bathed less frequently, but its skin must be clean. Remember that every time we bathe a dog, we eliminate from its coat the natural oils that keep it soft and shiny.

Since the coat is a significant factor in the beauty of the Havanese, we should take certain protective measures when we bathe this animal. First of all, if the coat is matted and knotted, the tangles should be eliminated before bathing. To facilitate that effort, we can prepare a solution of water and softener to be sprayed on the coat as we patiently untangle it with a brush or rake, taking care not to pull out the hairs. Only after completely untangling the coat can we bathe the dog. A dog

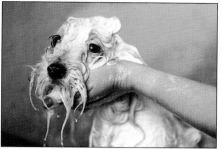

Take great care not to allow soap to irritate the Havanese's eyes. Likewise, a cotton wool bud in each ear protects them from water entering there.

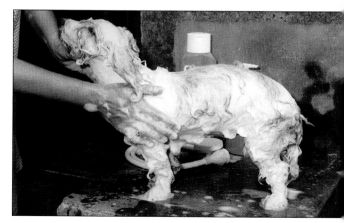

Never bathe an uncombed Havanese! In warmer climates, like Cuba, the Havanese needs to be bathed more frequently than in colder, damper places.

85

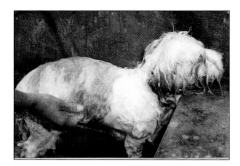

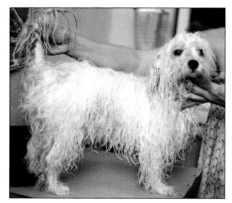

Thoroughly rinse all soap out of the coat. Residue from shampoo can cause irritation to the Havanese's skin. Dry the dog completely, using heavy towels and a blaster (on low). Do not hold the blaster too close to the dog's coat or you will burn him.

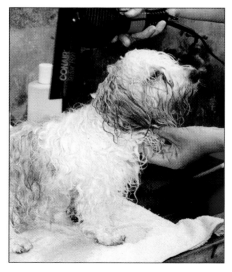

whose coat has been cared for won't have this problem and can be bathed without any previous preparation.

In Cuba, dogs are usually bathed in cold water because of the hot climate, though warm water is used in winter. In cold climates, the owner of a Havanese will regulate the temperature of the bath to the surroundings, so the water is neither too hot nor too cold.

A coconut aloe vera or some other oily shampoo will keep your pet's skin moist. Wet the dog thoroughly and apply shampoo to the trunk, tail, legs, feet

DID YOU KNOW?

Once you are sure that the dog is thoroughly rinsed, squeeze the excess water out of the coat with your hand and dry him with a heavy towel. You may choose to use a blaster on his coat or just let it dry naturally. In cold weather, never allow your dog outside with a wet coat.

There are 'dry bath' products on the market, which are sprays and powders intended for spot cleaning, that can be used between regular baths, if necessary. They are not substitutes for regular baths, but they are easy to use for touch-ups as they do not require rinsing.

and, finally, the head, being careful to keep the ears dry by inserting cotton wool beforehand. Rinse the dog thoroughly, then apply a softener mixed with water. This can be left on the coat to make it softer and more flexible for grooming or it can be rinsed off, at the owner's discretion.

On warmer days, your Havanese will enjoy bathing in the sun. Remember, these are native tropical dogs who live for sun! Sugar, owned by Barbara Monteagudo.

DID YOU KNOW?

The use of human soap products like shampoo, bubble bath and hand soap can be damaging to a dog's coat and skin. Human products are too strong and remove the protective oils coating the dog's hair and skin (making him water-resistant). Use only shampoo made especially for dogs and you may like to use a medicated shampoo which will always help to keep external parasites at bay.

Whilst the Havanese is dripping wet, squeeze the water gently from the tufts and let the animal shake itself thoroughly. Then towel its coat gently to retain the softener, if you decided to leave it on as recommended.

EYE CARE

Sometimes the Havanese tears and, as a result, accumulates dirt below its eyes. When this happens, rinse the eyes with a saline solution and dry each one with a separate piece of cotton wool. You can also use a small fine-toothed comb to keep the area clean.

Another method of keeping the face clean is to tie the head hair in a topknot so it doesn't fall over the eyes. This method should be monitored by a professional groomer so the hair isn't pulled or broken, especially if you plan to present your Havanese in a show, for the breed is not permitted to use topknots or any other kind of hair decoration.

EAR CARE

To clean the ears, you should first use a small tweezers like

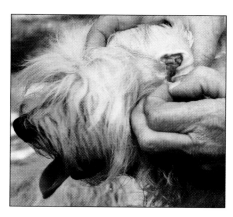

Clean ears are free of odour and secretion. Use a cotton wool bud and an ear cleanser to clean the outer part of the ear.

87

Remove tufts of hair that grow inside the ear. Be gentle so not to hurt your dog.

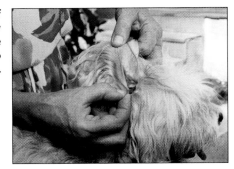

the forceps that surgeons use in hospital. With this little instrument, you can pull out the tufts of hair that grow inside the ears instead of using your fingers. These hairs should be removed carefully, never pulling on large tufts that will hurt your dog. You can clean the ears with a piece of cotton dipped in oil or an ear-cleaning solution purchased at a pet store. Clean, healthy ears are secretion- and odour-free. Ear problems require veterinary attention.

If you accustom your Havanese to nail clipping from puppyhood, he should accept the routine as an adult. Most dogs do not like the feeling of nail clipping, so proper introduction and training are key.

NAIL CLIPPING

As the Bichon Havanese grows and its coat becomes longer, the tufts of hair between the toes also grow, often until they totally cover the cushions of the feet. Our dog becomes uncomfortable as its posture and movement are affected. We need to check the feet systemati-

cally and cut out these tufts with a small scissors so that the cushions of the feet are completely hair-free.

The nails must also be monitored. A dog's nails should not touch the ground, much less curl into it. Your Havanese may file its nails naturally as it walks on hard surfaces, maintaining them at the proper length. If not, you will have to prevent discomfort and deformation of the feet by cutting the nails—-especially the nail of the supplementary toe, if that exists, for it should never touch the ground.

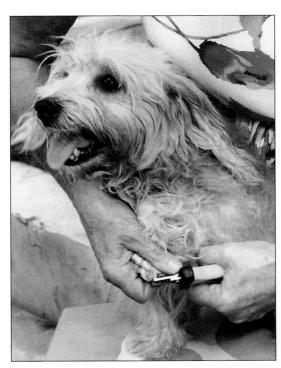

Use a nail trimmer for small dogs or cats and cut only the protruding part of the nail to avoid hurting the animal. First, raise your dog's foot and hold it against the light to observe what is called the quick, which is the vein that runs through the dog's nail. Do not cut into the quick or your dog will bleed. If the nails are black, cut a small triangle from the interior to the exterior edge of the nail no deeper than necessary. Should bleeding occur, press ice on the cut or press your thumb on the affected area until the bleeding stops. You may also apply a styptic powder or pencil.

It's best to accustom your dog to nail cutting and grooming as a pup so that it comes to accept them as a normal part of dog life. Moreover, systematic nail cutting helps the quick contract over time.

ANAL AREA

The anal glands should be systematically discharged to avoid infections and discomfort. It's best to do this while bathing the dog. Just raise the tail and use your thumb and index finger to press the anal area firmly until a dark brown secretion emerges. Wash and rinse the area thoroughly. It is also advisable to trim the hairs on and around the anus so that the area remains free for defecation.

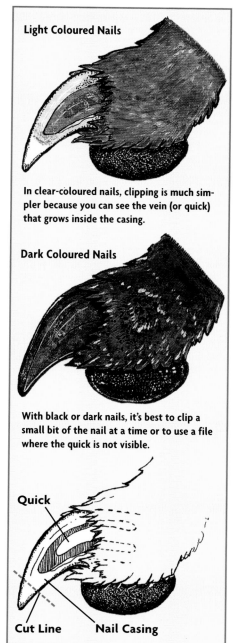

Light Coloured Nails

In clear-coloured nails, clipping is much simpler because you can see the vein (or quick) that grows inside the casing.

Dark Coloured Nails

With black or dark nails, it's best to clip a small bit of the nail at a time or to use a file where the quick is not visible.

Quick

Cut Line **Nail Casing**

Clip only the bottom portion of the nail as shown, avoiding the quick. If you cut into the quick, the nail will bleed and the dog will experience pain. A styptic pencil will stop the bleeding. Reassure the injured dog by talking quietly to him.

89

You should brush your Havanese's teeth at least once a week with a specially formulated toothpaste for dogs. Human toothpastes are too harsh for dogs' teeth.

TEETH

Once your Havanese has its permanent teeth, we should take measures to keep the mouth free of tartar buildup and other accumulations. It's a good idea to accustom the pup to having its teeth brushed weekly with a toothpaste for dogs. By the time it reaches adulthood, it will tolerate this kind of cleaning without objection.

A Havanese whose feet are properly groomed and whose nails are clipped will run with a smooth, easy gait. If your dog exercises frequently on hard surfaces, his nails will wear down naturally and you will not need to clip them as often.

Gnawing on bones, which should always be large, hard beef bones that can't be splintered or swallowed, is a natural way for dogs to clean their teeth. Pet stores also carry commercial products designed for this purpose, the most reliable of which are made of durable nylon.

Removing tufts from your Havanese's feet will help him to stand erect and proud, befitting his noble Cuban heritage.

If you notice that your dog's breath smells bad or its teeth have an accumulation of tartar, consult the veterinarian or a grooming professional about how best to eliminate these residues without harming the animal.

POSTURE

Although posture may seem somewhat unrelated to the topic of grooming, we've decided to refer to it in this chapter to help improve the proper overall image of your Bichon Havanese. By following the advice on nail cutting and tuft removal, you will help your dog's posture. And if you want to do a bit more for your pet, we can also recommend that you make a habit of feeding him

above floor level. The ideal is to locate the food at head height so the dog need not assume an uncomfortable posture to eat. If you begin doing this from the time he's a pup, raising the plate level according to his growth, you will note an improvement in the neck posture.

Another recourse is to stroke your dog on the underside of the neck rather than on top of the head when he comes to you. In the first place, it's more pleasing for him and, in the second place, you're training him to walk with his head up, for he will quickly learn that's when his master caresses him.

TRAVELLING WITH YOUR DOG

CAR TRAVEL

You should accustom your Bichon Havanese to riding in a car at an early age. You may or may not take him in the car often, but at the very least he will need to go to the vet and you do not want these trips to be traumatic for the dog or a big hassle for you. The safest way for a dog to ride in the car is in his crate. If he uses a crate in the house, you can use the same crate for travel.

Put the pup in the crate and see how he reacts. If he seems uneasy, you can have a passen-

The most acceptable, safest way of travelling with your Havanese in a car is in a crate. It is dangerous for the dog to have free access to all parts of the vehicle whilst it is moving.

ger hold him on his lap whilst you drive. Another option is a specially made safety harness for dogs, which straps the dog in much like a seat belt. Do not

DID YOU KNOW?

If you are going on a long motor trip with your dog, be sure the hotels are dog friendly. Many hotels do not accept dogs. Also take along some ice that can be thawed and offered to your dog if he becomes overheated. Most dogs like to lick ice.

let the dog roam loose in the vehicle—this is very dangerous! If you should stop short, your dog can be thrown and injured. If the dog starts climbing on you and pestering you whilst you are driving, you will not be able to concentrate on the road. It is an unsafe situation for everyone—human and canine.

For long trips, be prepared to stop to let the dog relieve

DID YOU KNOW?

When travelling, never let your dog off-lead in a strange area. Your dog could run away out of fear or decide to chase a passing chipmunk or cat or simply want to stretch his legs without restriction---you might never see your canine friend again.

91

himself. Bring along whatever you need to clean up after him. You should take along some paper kitchen towels and perhaps some old towelling for use should he have an accident in the car or suffer from travel sickness.

AIR TRAVEL

Whilst it is possible to take a dog on a flight within Britain, this is fairly unusual and advance permission is always required. The dog will be required to travel in a fibreglass crate and you should always check in advance with the airline regarding specific requirements. To help the dog be at ease, put one of his favourite toys in the crate with him. Do not feed the dog for at least six hours before the trip to minimise his need to relieve himself. However, certain regulations specify that water must always be made available to the dog in the crate.

Make sure your dog is properly identified and that your contact information appears on his ID tags and on his crate. Animals travel in a different area of the plane than human passengers so every rule must be strictly adhered to so as to prevent the risk of getting separated from your dog.

Travelling in the basket of a motorbike is not an acceptable mode of transport for the Havanese, but it sure makes a great photograph!

DID YOU KNOW?
However much your dog enjoys travelling, he should never be left alone in a car in warm weather, even with the windows left open. Heat builds up all too quickly and can cause suffering and tragedy. Even on a cloudy day one must always be aware that the sun can break through unexpectedly.

BOARDING

So you want to take a family holiday—and you want to include all members of the family. You would probably make arrangements for accommodations ahead of time anyway, but this is especially important when travelling with a dog. You do not want to make an overnight stop at the only place around for miles and find out that they do not allow dogs. Also, you do not want to reserve a place for your family without confirming that you are travelling with a dog because if it is against their policy you may not have a place to stay.

Alternatively, if you are travelling and choose not to bring your Bichon Havanese, you will have to make arrangements for him whilst you are away. Some options are to take him to a neighbour's house to stay whilst you are gone, to have a trusted neighbour stop by often or stay at your house, or bring your dog to a reputable boarding kennel. If you choose to board him at a kennel, you should visit in advance to see the facility, how clean they are and where

Havaneses are willing passengers and look forward to a Sunday drive. Be sure that your dogs are secured properly in your car before driving. You might consider a doggie harness that attaches to the safety belts of the rear passenger seat if you'd rather not use a crate. Sugar and Ambar, owned by Barbara Monteagudo.

Should you find it necessary to board your Havanese whilst you are on holiday, locate a facility with clean accommodations and a friendly staff.

DID YOU KNOW?

If your dog gets lost, he is not able to ask for directions home.

Identification tags fastened to the collar give important information—the dog's name, the owner's name, the owner's address and a telephone number where the owner can be reached. This makes it easy for whoever finds the dog to contact the owner and arrange to have the dog returned. An added advantage is that a person will be more likely to approach a lost dog who has ID tags on his collar; it tells the person that this is somebody's pet rather than a stray. This is the easiest and fastest method of identification provided that the tags stay on the collar and the collar stays on the dog.

the dogs are kept. Talk to some of the employees and see how they treat the dogs—do they spend time with the dogs, play with them, exercise them, etc.? Also find out the kennel's policy on vaccinations and what they require. This is for all of the dogs' safety, since when dogs are kept together, there is a greater risk of diseases being passed from dog to dog.

IDENTIFICATION

Your Bichon Havanese is your valued companion and friend. That is why you always keep a close eye on him and you have made sure that he cannot

Your Havanese's ID tags should be securely attached to his collar.

DID YOU KNOW?

As puppies become more and more expensive, especially those puppies of high quality for showing and/or breeding, they have a greater chance of being stolen. The usual collar dog tag is, of course, easily removed. But there are two techniques that have become widely utilised for identification.

The puppy microchip implantation involves the injection of a small microchip, about the size of a corn kernel, under the skin of the dog. If your dog shows up at a clinic or shelter, or is offered for resale under less than savory circumstances, it can be positively identified by the microchip. The microchip is scanned and a registry quickly identifies you as the owner. This is not only protection against theft, but should the dog run away or go chasing a squirrel and get lost, you have a fair chance of getting it back.

Tattooing is done on various parts of the dog, from its belly to its cheeks. The number tattooed can be your telephone number or any other number which you can easily memorise. When professional dog thieves see a tattooed dog, they usually lose interest in it. Both microchipping and tattooing can be done at your local veterinary clinic. For the safety of our dogs, no laboratory facility or dog broker will accept a tattooed dog as stock.

escape from the garden or wriggle out of his collar and run away from you. However, accidents can happen and there may come a time when your dog unexpectedly gets separated from you. If this unfortunate event should occur, the first thing on your mind will be finding him. Proper identification, including an ID tag, a tattoo, and possibly a microchip, will increase the chances of his being returned to you safely and quickly.

DID YOU KNOW?

You have a valuable dog. If the dog is lost or stolen you would undoubtedly become extremely upset. If you encounter a lost dog, notify the police or the local animal shelter.

The Havanese is the favourite pet in Cuba. This one is at home on the farm in front of Cuba's other famous export, tobacco. The barn in the background is where the tobacco is dried.

HOUSEBREAKING AND TRAINING YOUR
Bichon Havanese

Puppies learn from their mother in a natural way. But when you bring a Havanese into your house, you want to teach it habits and customs appropriate to your family life. Indeed you also want to give it some basic obedience training so it can walk correctly on leash, and come or sit on command.

Basic training will be useful for your Havanese and also for you. As we noted earlier, the dog is a pack animal, programmed by nature to lead or to follow one who, in this case and under all circumstances, has to be you. As the leader, you give your dog a feeling of security and protection and the guidance it needs. A dog

left to its own devices is not a balanced or happy animal.

A Havanese's education begins the very instant you bring it home. At first, your pup should be confined to its own area. To avoid accidents and destructive behaviour, an animal should be housebroken before it is given the run of your home. Teach your Havanese by habit, never by hitting, that it has a fixed place to eat, a fixed place to urinate and defecate and a fixed place to sleep.

It is also important to teach your dog to respond to his name. Call him by name to feed him or pet him, but never call him by name when you're going to scold him. For that, there's just one word, spoken firmly and definitively: NO!

You should recognise that the puppy will do everything possible to control you, which you cannot permit. You have to impose your will, little by little; not by force, but by making him understand. To make a dog understand us, we must learn to put ourselves in its place and not presume—as many people

do—that the dog is human and lives in our world. That is impossible. The essential qualities for teaching are patience and perseverance. Repeat the command until the dog understands what is expected of him.

In giving commands, we should use short, clear words that are always the same. For example, when we call the dog, we can't alternate between 'Come' and 'Here'. Choose one and keep it so you won't confuse him. Also, speak, don't scream your commands.

Personal experience has taught me that one factor in the man-dog relationship most owners neglect, even though it is of primary importance and utility, is talking to your dog. Verbal communication is an excellent method of directing your dog with the guarantee that you will always be obeyed. But you have to know how. The first thing to do is relax and pay no attention to what others might think of you. (I know men who don't like to sweet-talk their dogs because

A well-trained Havanese is a joy to his owner. This is Cuban champion Esmerelda de la Giraldilla, owned by Merita Batista and Annia Barroso, in front of La Chorrera Castle in Havana.

they consider it unmasculine.) Talk to your dog about everything that affects him. If you're going to give him medicine, first talk to him softly and lovingly to calm him. The same thing if you're going to groom him. Show him the comb, let him smell it, tell him it won't hurt...and you'll see the results.

In many cases, we humans act as if the dog were not a living creature with concerns and fears. We think we have the right to do what we want with him: check his body, poke into his ears, or——without any pre-amble—-start clipping his nails or stick a needle in his skin to vaccinate him. Put yourself in your dog's place and imagine if someone treated you that way. Wouldn't you feel violated? How much better it would be if you were first told

DID YOU KNOW?

Mealtime should be a peaceful time for your puppy. Do not put his food and water bowls in a high-traffic area in the house. For example, give him his own little corner of the kitchen where he can eat undisturbed and where he will not be under foot. Do not allow small children or other family members to disrupt the pup when he is eating.

DID YOU KNOW?

To a dog's way of thinking, your hands are like his mouth in terms of a defence mechanism. If you squeeze him too tightly, he might just bite you because that would be his normal response. This is not aggressive biting and, although all biting should be discouraged, you need the discipline in learning how to handle your dog.

in detail what to expect. Well, the same is true of your dog. We should talk to him softly, with love, so he understands us and our intentions. Of course, he won't understand the words, but he will understand our tone of voice and will respond with confidence and tranquillity. This confidence is just what we need to be able to direct him easily, without verbal or physical aggression. Try it, and when you become accustomed to this method, perhaps you'll agree with me that most of us operate on the absurd pretext of being understood without offering explanations, and this is as true in human relations as in relations with your animals.

The most appropriate age to start basic training is three months, before the dog acquires bad habits. Our goal is to have our Havanese obey us cheerfully, with the express desire of pleasing us, and not out of fear.

You may want to look into the training courses available in many books and institutions that offer such instruction. Whatever method you choose to follow, we can only add that a good teacher should know when to reward and when to punish. Punishment does not mean hitting the dog, but rather reprimanding him with a firm NO when he does something improper. A reward should be given to reinforce any positive conduct: each time your Havanese does something right, caress him and praise him. Better than any food treat, the best reward a dog can have is his master's love and approval.

HOUSEBREAKING

You can train a puppy to relieve itself wherever you choose, but this must be somewhere suitable. You should bear in mind from the outset that when your puppy is old enough to go out in public places, any canine

DID YOU KNOW?

Dogs are sensitive to their master's moods and emotions. Use your voice wisely when communicating with your dog. Never raise your voice at your dog unless you are angry and trying to correct him. 'Barking' at your dog can become as meaningless as 'dogspeak' is to you. Think before you bark!

deposits must be removed at once. You will always have to carry with you a small plastic bag or 'poop-scoop.'

Outdoor training includes such surfaces as grass, dirt and cement. Indoor training usually means training your dog to newspaper.

When deciding on the surface and location that you will want your Bichon Havanese to use, be sure it is going to be permanent. Training your dog to grass and then changing your mind two months later is extremely difficult for both dog and owner.

Teach your Havanese the rules of your household from puppyhood. You cannot allow your dog to sit on the furniture outdoors and then forbid him to sit on the furniture inside your home. Consistency pays off in dog training.

101

If you acclimate your Havanese to relieve himself on grass, this is the surface that he will always seek out. Grass is the most common choice since it is available most anywhere you go.

Next, choose the command you will use each and every time you want your puppy to void. 'Go hurry up' and 'Toilet' are examples of commands commonly used by dog owners.

Get in the habit of giving the puppy your chosen relief command before you take him out. That way, when he becomes an adult, you will be able to determine if he wants to go out when you ask him. A confirmation will be signs of interest, wagging his tail, watching you intently, going to the door, etc.

PUPPY'S NEEDS
Puppy needs to relieve himself after play periods, after each meal, after he has been sleeping and any time he indicates that he is looking for a place to urinate or defecate.

The urinary and intestinal tract muscles of very young puppies are not fully developed. Therefore, like human babies, puppies need to relieve themselves frequently.

Take your puppy out often—every hour for an eight-week-old, for example, and always immediately after sleeping and eating. The older the puppy, the less often he will need to relieve himself. Finally, as a mature healthy adult, he will require only three to five relief trips per day.

HOUSING
Since the types of housing and control you provide for your puppy has a direct relationship on the success of housetraining, we consider the various aspects of both before we begin training.

DID YOU KNOW?
Dogs will do anything for your attention. If you reward the dog when he is calm and resting, you will develop a well-mannered dog. If, on the other hand, you greet your dog excitedly and encourage him to wrestle and roughhouse with you, the dog will greet you the same way and you will have a hyper dog on your hands.

Canine Development Schedule

It is important to understand how and at what age a puppy develops into adulthood. If you are a puppy owner, consult the following Canine Development Schedule to determine the stage of development your Bichon Havanese puppy is currently experiencing. This knowledge will help you as you work with the puppy in the weeks and months ahead.

Period	Age	Characteristics
FIRST TO THIRD	BIRTH TO SEVEN WEEKS	Puppy needs food, sleep and warmth, and responds to simple and gentle touching. Needs mother for security and disciplining. Needs litter mates for learning and interacting with other dogs. Pup learns to function within a pack and learns pack order of dominance. Begin socialising with adults and children for short periods. Begins to become aware of its environment.
FOURTH	EIGHT TO TWELVE WEEKS	Brain is fully developed. Needs socialising with outside world. Remove from mother and littermates. Needs to change from canine pack to human pack. Human dominance necessary. Fear period occurs between 8 and 16 weeks. Avoid fright and pain.
FIFTH	THIRTEEN TO SIXTEEN WEEKS	Training and formal obedience should begin. Less association with other dogs, more with people, places, situations. Period will pass easily if you remember this is pup's change-to-adolescence time. Be firm and fair. Flight instinct prominent. Permissiveness and over-disciplining can do permanent damage. Praise for good behaviour.
JUVENILE	FOUR TO EIGHT MONTHS	Another fear period about 7 to 8 months of age. It passes quickly, but be cautious of fright and pain. Sexual maturity reached. Dominant traits established. Dog should understand sit, down, come and stay by now.

NOTE: THESE ARE APPROXIMATE TIME FRAMES. ALLOW FOR INDIVIDUAL DIFFERENCES IN PUPPIES.

HOW MANY TIMES A DAY?

AGE	RELIEF TRIPS
To 14 weeks	10
14–22 weeks	8
22–32 weeks	6
Adulthood	4
(dog stops growing)	

These are estimates, of course, but they are a guide to the MINIMUM opportunities a dog should have each day to relieve itself.

Bringing a new puppy home and turning him loose in your house can be compared to turning a child loose in a sports arena and telling the child that the place is all his! The sheer enormity of the place would be too much for him to handle.

Instead, offer the puppy clearly defined areas where he can play, sleep, eat

DID YOU KNOW?

Dogs are the most honourable animals in existence. They consider another species (humans) as their own. They interface with you. You are their leader. Puppies perceive children to be on their level: their actions around small children are different than their behaviour around their adult masters.

and live. A room of the house where the family gathers is the most obvious choice. Puppies are social animals and need to feel a part of the pack right from the start. Hearing your voice, watching you whilst you are doing things and smelling you nearby are all positive reinforcers that he is now a member of your pack. Usually a family room, the kitchen or a nearby adjoining

TRAINING TIP

Stand up straight and authoritatively when giving your dog commands. Do not issue commands when lying on the floor or lying on your back on the sofa. If you are on your hands and knees when you give a command, your dog will think you are positioning yourself to play.

breakfast area is ideal for providing safety and security for both puppy and owner.

Within that room there should be a smaller area which the puppy can call his own. An alcove, a wire play pen or a fenced (not boarded!) corner from which he can view the activities of his new family will be fine. Dogs are, by nature, clean animals and will not remain close to their relief areas unless forced to do so. In those cases, they then become dirty dogs and usually remain that way for life.

The designated area should be lined with clean bedding and a toy. Water must always be available, in a non-spill container.

CONTROL

By control, we mean helping the puppy to create a lifestyle pattern that will be compatible to that of his human pack (YOU!). Just as we guide little children to learn our way of life, we must show the puppy when it is time to play, eat, sleep, exercise and even entertain himself.

Your puppy should always sleep in a designated space.

He should also learn that, during times of household confusion and excessive human activity such as at breakfast when family members are preparing for the day, he can play by himself in relative safety and comfort in his designated area. Each time you leave the puppy alone, he should understand exactly where he is to stay. You can gradually increase the time he is left alone to get him used to it.

A wire crate offers your Havanese many advantages. In warmer climes, the wire crate is ideal for ventilation. Most Havaneses like to be able to see what's going on about them.

If convenient or desirable, section off a part of your patio for your Havanese to use to relieve himself. If he is placed in the penned off area whenever you want him to relieve himself, he will understand your intentions.

Puppies are chewers. They cannot tell the difference between lamp cords, television wires, shoes, table legs, etc. Chewing into a television wire, for example, can be fatal to the puppy whilst a shorted wire can start a fire in the house.

If the puppy chews on the arm of the chair when he is alone, you will probably disci-

pline him angrily when you get home. Thus, he makes the association that your coming home means he is going to be punished. (He will not remember chewing up the chair and is incapable of making the association of the discipline with his naughty deed.)

Other times of excitement, such as family parties, etc., can be fun for the puppy providing he can view the activities from the security of his designated area. He is not under-

foot and he is not being fed all sorts of titbits that will probably cause him stomach distress, yet he still feels a part of the fun.

SCHEDULE
A puppy should be taken to his relief area each time he is released from his designated area, after meals, after a play session, when he first awakens in the morning (at age eight weeks, this can mean 5 a.m.!). The puppy will indicate that he's

TRAINING TIP
Do not carry your dog to his toilet area. Lead him there on a leash or, better yet, encourage him to follow you to the spot. If you start carrying him to his spot, you might end up doing this routine forever and your dog will have the satisfaction of having trained YOU.

ready 'to go' by circling or sniffing busily—-do not misinterpret these signs. For a puppy less than ten weeks of age, a routine of taking him out every hour is necessary. As the puppy grows, he will be able to wait for longer periods of time.

Keep trips to his relief area short. Stay no more than five or six minutes and then return to the house. If he goes during that time, praise him lavishly and take him indoors immediately. If he does not, but he has an accident when you go back indoors, pick him up immediately, say 'No! No!' and return to his relief area. Wait a few minutes, then return to the house again. never

hit a puppy or rub his face in urine or excrement when he has an accident!

Once indoors, put the puppy in his crate until you have had time to clean up his accident. Then release him to the family area and watch him more closely than before. Chances are, his accident was a result of your not picking up his signal or waiting too long before offering him the opportunity to relieve himself. Never hold a grudge against the puppy for accidents.

Let the puppy learn that going outdoors means it is time to relieve himself, not

DID YOU KNOW?
Practice Makes Perfect!
• Have training lessons with your dog every day in several short segments—three to five times a day for a few minutes at a time is ideal.
• Do not have long practice sessions. The dog will become easily bored.
• Never practice when you are tired, ill, worried or in an otherwise negative mood. This will transmit to the dog and may have an adverse effect on its performance.

Think fun, short and above all POSITIVE! End each session on a high note, rather than a failed exercise, and make sure to give a lot of praise. Enjoy the training and help your dog enjoy it, too.

Be an ideal dog owner: clean up after your dog whether in a public place or in your own garden.

THE SUCCESS METHOD
6 Steps to Successful Crate Training

1 Tell the puppy 'Crate time!' and place him in the crate with a small treat (a piece of cheese or half of a biscuit). Let him stay in the crate for five minutes while you are in the same room. Then release him and praise lavishly. Never release him when he is fussing. Wait until he is quiet before you let him out.

2 Repeat Step 1 several times a day.

3 The next day, place the puppy in the crate as before. Let him stay there for ten minutes. Do this several times.

4 Continue building time in five-minute increments until the puppy stays in his crate for 30 minutes with you in the room. Always take him to his relief area after prolonged periods in his crate.

5 Now go back to Step 1 and let the puppy stay in his crate for five minutes, this time while you are out of the room.

6 Once again, build crate time in five-minute increments with you out of the room. When the puppy will stay willingly in his crate (he may even fall asleep!) for 30 minutes with you out of the room, he will be ready to stay in it for several hours at a time.

TRAINING TIP

Most of all, be consistent. Always take your dog to the same location, always use the same command, and always have him on lead when he is in his relief area, unless a fenced-in garden is available.

By following the Success Method, your puppy will be completely house-trained by the time his muscle and brain development reach maturity. Keep in mind that small breeds usually mature faster than large breeds, but all puppies should be trained by six months of age.

play. Once trained, he will be able to play indoors and out and still differentiate between the times for play versus the times for relief.

Help him develop regular hours for naps, being alone, playing by himself and just resting, all in his crate. Encourage him to entertain himself whilst you are busy with your activities. Let him learn that having you near is comforting, but it is not your main purpose in life to provide him with undivided attention.

Each time you put a puppy in his own area, use the same command, whatever suits best.

An impressionable, young Havanese puppy will rely on you for all his needs. This includes his instruction. If you are confused about how to housetrain your dog, imagine how he must feel!

Soon, he will run to his crate or special area when he hears you say those words.

Crate training provides safety for you, the puppy and the home. It also provides the puppy with a feeling of security, and that helps the puppy achieve self-confidence and clean habits.

Remember that one of the primary ingredients in house-

training your puppy is control. Regardless of your lifestyle, there will always be occasions when you will need to have a place where your dog can stay and be happy and safe. Training is the answer for now and in the future.

In conclusion, a few key elements are really all you need for a successful house training method—consistency, frequency, praise, control and supervision. By following these procedures with a normal, healthy puppy, you and the puppy will soon be past the stage of 'accidents' and ready to move on to a full and rewarding life together.

Your Havanese will do his best to express his desires: 'I want to go out now!'

ROLES OF DISCIPLINE, REWARD AND PUNISHMENT

Discipline, training one to act in accordance with rules, brings order to life. It is as simple as that. Without discipline, particularly in a group society, chaos reigns supreme and the group will eventually perish. Humans and canines are social animals and need some form of discipline in order to function effectively. They must procure food, protect their home base and their young and reproduce to keep the species going.

If there were no discipline in the lives of social animals, they would eventually die from starvation and/or predation by other stronger animals.

In the case of domestic canines, dogs need discipline in their lives in order to understand how their pack (you and other family members) functions and how they must act in order to survive.

A large humane society in

a highly populated area recently surveyed dog owners regarding their satisfaction with their relationships with their dogs. People who had trained their dogs were 75% more satisfied with their pets than those who had never trained their dogs.

Dr. Edward Thorndike, a psychologist, established *Thorndike's Theory of Learning*, which states that a behaviour that results in a pleasant event tends to be repeated. A behaviour that results in an unpleasant event tends not to be repeated. It is this theory on which training methods are based today. For example, if you manipulate a dog to perform a specific behaviour and reward him for doing it, he is likely to do it again because he enjoyed the end result.

Occasionally, punishment, a penalty inflicted for an offence, is necessary. The best type of punishment often comes from an outside source. For example, a child is told not to touch the stove because he may get burned. He disobeys and touches the stove. In doing so, he receives a burn. From that time on, he respects the heat of the stove and avoids contact with it. Therefore, a behaviour that results in an unpleasant event tends not to be repeated.

A good example of a dog learning the hard way is the dog who chases the house cat. He is told many times to leave the cat alone, yet he persists in teasing the cat. Then, one day he begins chasing the cat but the cat turns and swipes a claw across the dog's face, leaving him with a painful gash on his nose. The final result is that the dog stops chasing the cat.

TRAINING EQUIPMENT
COLLAR AND LEAD

For a Bichon Havanese the collar and lead that you use for training must be one with which you are easily able to work, not too heavy for the dog and perfectly safe. For the Havanese, a light nylon lead and collar is perfectly suitable.

TREATS

Assuming that your Havanese is performing on command primarily to please you, his owner, you may wish to incorporate food rewards into your training routine. Have a bag of treats on hand. Something nutritious and easy to swallow works best. Use a soft treat, a chunk of cheese or a piece of cooked chicken rather than a dry biscuit. By the time the dog gets done chewing a dry treat, he will forget why he is being rewarded in the first place! Using food rewards will not teach a dog to beg at the table—the only way to teach a dog to beg at the table is to give him food from the table. In training, rewarding the dog with a food treat will help him associate praise and the treats with learning new behaviours that obviously please his owner.

TRAINING BEGINS:
ASK THE DOG A QUESTION

In order to teach your dog anything, you must first get his attention. After all, he cannot learn anything if he is looking away from you with his mind on something else.

To get his attention, ask him, 'School?' and immediately walk over to him and give him a treat as you tell him 'Good dog.' Wait a minute or two and repeat the routine, this time with a treat in your hand as you approach within a foot of the dog. Do not go directly to him, but stop about a foot short of him and hold out the treat as you ask, 'School?' He will see you approaching with a treat in your

(FACING PAGE) Whilst your Havanese should obey your commands out of love and respect for you, many trainers rely upon food treats to 'bribe' the dog to pay attention. Use treats wisely—or you will not be in control, the cheese will!

Do not attempt to train your dog in an area where there are many distractions—even if the distractions are as tiny as a flea!

> **TRAINING TIP**
> Use treats to bribe your dog into desired behaviour. Try small pieces of hard cheese or freeze-dried liver. Never offer chocolate as it has toxic qualities for dogs.

hand and most likely begin walking toward you. As you meet, give him the treat and praise again.

The third time, ask the question, have a treat in your hand and walk only a short distance toward the dog so that he must walk almost all the way to you. As he reaches you, give him the treat and praise again.

By this time, the dog will probably be getting the idea that if he pays attention to you, especially when you ask that question, it will pay off in treats and fun activities for him. In other words, he learns that 'school'

> **DID YOU KNOW?**
> Dogs do not understand our language. They can be trained to react to a certain sound, at a certain volume. If you say 'No, Oliver' in a very soft pleasant voice it will not have the same meaning as 'No, Oliver!!' when you shout it as loud as you can. You should never use the dog's name during a reprimand, just the command NO!! Since dogs don't understand words, comics use dogs trained with opposite meanings. Thus, when the comic commands his dog to SIT the dog will stand up; and vice versa.

means doing fun things with you that result in treats and positive attention for him.

Remember that the dog does not understand your verbal language, he only recognises sounds. Your question translates to a series of sounds for him, and those sounds become the signal to go to you and pay attention; if he does, he will get to interact with you plus receive treats and praise

THE BASIC COMMANDS
TEACHING SIT
Now that you have the dog's attention, attach his lead and hold it in your left hand and a food treat in your right. Place your food hand at the dog's nose and let him lick the treat but not take it from you. Say 'Sit' and slowly raise your food hand from in front of the dog's nose up over his head so that he is looking at the ceiling. As he bends his

Reward your dog with petting and praise when he has obeyed your command. Do not overdo it or the dog will lose focus on the lesson at hand.

TRAINING TIP
Play fetch games with your puppy in an enclosed area where he can retrieve his toy and bring it back to you. Always use a toy or object designated just for this purpose. Never use a shoe, sock or other item he may later confuse with those in your closet or underneath your chair.

TRAINING TIP
Never train your pup when you are mad or in a surly mood. Dogs are very sensitive to human feelings, and if your dog senses that you are angry or upset, he will connect your anger with his training and learn to resent or fear his training sessions.

head upward, he will have to bend his knees to maintain his balance. As he bends his knees, he will assume a sit position. At that point, release the food treat and praise lavishly with comments such as 'Good dog! Good sit!', etc. Remember to always

Use food to teach new commands. Once the dog associates the word with the desired response, food should not be the key motivating factor.

praise enthusiastically, because dogs relish verbal praise from their owners and feel so proud of themselves whenever they accomplish a behaviour.

You will not use food forever in getting the dog to obey your commands. Food is only used to teach new behaviours, and once the dog knows what you want when you give a specific command, you will wean him off of the food treats but still maintain the verbal praise. After all, you will always have your voice with you, and there will be many times when you have no food rewards but expect the dog to obey.

Teaching Down

Teaching the down exercise is easy when you understand how the dog perceives the down position, and it is very difficult when you do not. Dogs perceive the down position as a submissive one, therefore teaching the down exercise using a forceful method can sometimes make the dog develop such a fear of the down that he either runs away when you say 'Down' or he attempts to snap at the person who tries to force him down.

Have the dog sit close along-

The sit/stay exercise develops from the proper execution of the sit command. Remember to use the food treat sparingly so that the dog doesn't confuse lesson time with meal time!

Keep talking softly to the dog, saying things like, 'Do you want this treat? You can do this, good dog.' Your reassuring tone of voice will help calm the dog as he tries to follow the food hand in order to get the treat.

When the dog's elbows touch the floor, release the food and praise softly. Try to get the dog to maintain that down position for several seconds before you let him sit up again. The goal here is to get the dog to settle down and not feel threatened in the down position.

TEACHING STAY
It is easy to teach the dog to stay in either a sit or a down position. Again, we use food and praise during the

side your left leg, facing in the same direction as you are. Hold the lead in your left hand and a food treat in your right. Now place your left hand lightly on the top of the dog's shoulders where they meet above the spinal cord. Do not push down on the dog's shoulders; simply rest your left hand there so you can guide the dog to lie down close to your left leg rather than to swing away from your side when he drops.

Now place the food hand at the dog's nose, say 'Down' very softly (almost a whisper), and slowly lower the food hand to the dog's front feet. When the food hand reaches the floor, begin moving it forward along the floor in front of the dog.

DID YOU KNOW?
By providing sleeping and resting quarters that fit the dog, and offering frequent opportunities to relieve himself outside his quarters, the puppy quickly learns that the outdoors (or the newspaper if you are training him to paper) is the place to go when he needs to urinate or defecate. It also reinforces his innate desire to keep his sleeping quarters clean. This, in turn, helps develop the muscle control that will eventually produce a dog with clean living habits.

teaching process as we help the dog to understand exactly what it is that we are expecting him to do.

To teach the sit/stay, start with the dog sitting on your left side as before and hold the lead in your left hand. Have a food treat in your right hand and place your food hand at the dog's nose. Say 'Stay' and step out on your right foot to stand directly in front of the dog, toe to toe, as he licks and nibbles the treat. Be sure to keep his head facing upward to maintain the sit position. Count to five and then swing around to stand next to the dog again with him on your left. As soon as you get back to the original position, release the food and praise lavishly.

To teach the down/stay, do the down as previously described. As soon as the dog lies down, say 'Stay' and step out on your right foot just as you did in the sit/stay. Count to five and then return to stand beside the dog with him on your left side. Release the treat and praise as always.

Within a week or ten days, you can begin to add a bit of distance between you and your dog when you leave him. When you do, use your left hand open with the palm facing the dog as a stay signal, much the same as the hand signal a police officer uses to stop traffic at an intersection. Hold the food treat in your right hand as before, but this time the food is not touching the dog's nose. He will watch the food hand and quickly learn that he is going to get that treat as soon as you return to his side.

When you can stand 1 metre away from your dog for 30 seconds, you can then begin building time and distance in both stays. Eventually, the dog can be expected to remain in the stay position for prolonged periods of time until you return to him or call him to you. Always praise lavishly when he stays.

TEACHING COME

If you make teaching 'come' a fun experience, you should never have a 'student' that does not love the game or that fails to come when called. The secret, it seems, is never to teach the word 'come.'

At times when an owner most wants his dog to come when called, the owner is likely upset or anxious and he allows these feelings to come through in the tone of his voice when he calls his dog. Hearing that desperation in his owner's voice, the dog fears the results of going to him and therefore either disobeys outright or runs in the opposite direction. The secret, therefore, is to teach the dog a game and, when you want him to come to you, simply play

TRAINING TIP

When calling the dog, do not say 'Come.' Say things like, 'Rover, where are you? See if you can find me! I have a cookie for you!' Keep up a constant line of chatter with coaxing sounds and frequent questions such as, 'Where are you?' The dog will learn to follow the sound of your voice to locate you and receive his reward.

TRAINING TIP

Never call your dog to come to you for a correction or scold him when he reaches you. That is the quickest way to turn a 'Come' command into 'Go away fast!' Dogs think only in the present tense and he will connect the scolding with coming to his master, not with the misbehaviour of a few moments earlier.

the game. It is practically a no-fail solution!

To begin, have several members of your family take a few food treats and each go into a different room in the house. Take turns calling the dog, and each person should celebrate the dog's finding him with a treat and lots of happy praise. When a person calls the dog, he is actually inviting the dog to find him and get a treat as a reward for 'winning.'

A few turns of the 'Where are you?' game and the dog will figure out that everyone is playing the game and that each person has a big celebration awaiting his success at locating them. Once he learns to love the game, simply calling out 'Where are you?' will bring him running from wherever he is when he hears that all-important question.

The come command is recognised as one of the most important things to teach a dog, but there are trainers who work with thousands of dogs and never teach the actual word 'Come.' Yet these dogs will race to respond to a person who uses the dog's name followed by 'Where are you?' For example, a woman has a 12-year-old companion dog who went blind, but who never fails to locate her owner when asked, 'Where are you?'

Children particularly love to play this game with their dogs. Children can hide in smaller places like a shower or bathtub, behind a bed or under a table. The dog needs to work a little bit harder to find these hiding places, but when he does he loves to celebrate with a treat and a tussle with a favourite youngster.

A Havanese heeling at its handler's side is completely in tune to the direction and tempo of the handler.

TEACHING HEEL

Heeling means that the dog walks beside the owner without pulling. It takes time and patience on the owner's part to succeed at teaching the dog that he (the owner) will not proceed unless the dog is walking calmly beside him. Pulling out ahead on the lead is definitely not acceptable.

Begin with holding the lead in your left hand as the dog sits beside your left leg. Move the loop end of the lead to your right hand but keep your left hand short on the lead so it keeps the dog in close next to you.

Say 'Heel' and step forward on your left foot. Keep the dog close to you and take three steps. Stop and have the dog sit next to you in what we now call the 'heel position.' Praise verbally, but do not touch the dog. Hesitate a moment and begin again with 'Heel,' taking three steps and stopping, at which point the dog is told to sit again.

> **TRAINING TIP**
> If you are walking your dog and he suddenly stops and looks straight into your eyes, ignore him. Pull the leash and lead him into the direction you want to walk.

Your goal here is to have the dog walk those three steps without pulling on the lead. When he will walk calmly beside you for three steps without pulling, increase the number of steps you take to five. When he will walk politely beside you whilst you take five steps, you can increase the length of your walk to ten steps. Keep increasing the length of your stroll until the dog will walk quietly beside you without pulling as long as you want him to heel. When you stop heeling, indicate to the dog that the exercise is over by verbally praising as you pet him and say 'OK, good dog.' The 'OK' is used as a release word meaning that the exercise is finished and the dog is free to relax.

If you are dealing with a dog who insists on pulling you around, simply 'put on your brakes' and stand your ground until the dog realises that the two of you are not going anywhere until he is beside you and moving at your pace, not his. It may take some time just standing there to convince the dog that you are the leader and you will be the one to decide on the direction and speed of your travel.

Each time the dog looks up at you or slows down to give a slack lead between the two of you, quietly praise him and say, 'Good heel. Good dog.' Eventually, the dog will begin to respond and within a few days he will be walking politely beside you without pulling on the lead. At first, the training sessions should be kept short and very positive; soon the dog will be able to walk nicely with you for increasingly longer distances. Remember also to give the dog free time and the opportunity to run and play when you are done with heel practice.

WEANING OFF FOOD IN TRAINING
Food is used in training new behaviours. Once the dog understands what behaviour goes with a specific command, it is time to start weaning him off the food treats. At first, give a treat after each exercise. Then, start to give a treat only

DID YOU KNOW?
A basic obedience beginner's class usually lasts for six to eight weeks. Dog and owner attend an hour-long lesson once a week and practice for a few minutes, several times a day, each day at home. If done properly, the whole procedure will result in a well-mannered dog and an owner who delights in living with a pet that is eager to please and enjoys doing things with his owner.

after every other exercise. Mix up the times when you offer a food reward and the times when you only offer praise so that the dog will never know when he is going to receive both food and praise and when he is going to receive only praise. This is called a variable ratio reward system and it proves successful because there is always the chance that the owner will produce a treat, so the dog never stops trying for that reward. No matter what, ALWAYS give verbal praise.

OBEDIENCE CLASSES

It is a good idea to enrol in an obedience class if one is available in your area. If yours is a show dog, ringcraft classes would be more appropriate.. Many areas have dog clubs that offer basic obedience training as well as preparatory classes for obedience competition. There are also local dog trainers who offer similar classes.

At obedience trials, dogs can earn titles at various levels of competition. The beginning levels of competition include basic behaviours such as sit, down, heel, etc. The more advanced levels of competition include jumping, retrieving, scent discrimination and signal work. The advanced levels require a dog and owner to put a lot of time and effort into their training and the titles that can be earned at these levels of competition are very prestigious.

Do not pull your Havanese when training him to heel. He should not associate the heel exercise with an unpleasant experience.

121

OTHER ACTIVITIES FOR LIFE

Whether a dog is trained in the structured environment of a class or alone with his owner at home, there are many activities that can bring fun and rewards to both owner and dog once they have mastered basic control.

Teaching the dog to help out around the home, in the garden or on the farm provides great satisfaction to both dog and owner. In addition, the dog's help makes life a little easier for

DID YOU KNOW?
Occasionally, a dog and owner who have not attended formal classes have been able to earn entry-level titles by obtaining competition rules and regulations from a local kennel club and practising on their own to a degree of perfection. Obtaining the higher level titles, however, almost always requires extensive training under the tutelage of experienced instructors. In addition, the more difficult levels require more specialised equipment whereas the lower levels do not.

Havaneses trained for the show ring must respond effortlessly to their handlers' leads. For show dogs, heeling is an obvious requirement if the dogs are to display proper gait.

his owner and raises his stature as a valued companion to his family. It helps give the dog a purpose by occupying his mind and providing an outlet for his energy.

If you are interested in participating in organised competition with your Havanese, there are activities other than obedience in which you and your dog can become involved. Agility is a popular and fun sport where dogs run through an obstacle course that includes various jumps, tunnels and other exercises to test the dog's speed and coordination. The owners run through the course beside their dogs to give commands and to guide them through the course. Although competitive, the focus is on fun—it's fun to do, fun to watch, and great exercise.

HEALTH CARE OF YOUR
Bichon Havanese

Dogs suffer many of the same physical illnesses as people. They might even share many of the same psychological problems. Since people usually know more about human diseases than canine maladies, many of the terms used in this chapter will be familiar but not necessarily those used by veterinary surgeons. We will use the term x-ray, instead of the more acceptable term radiograph. We will also use the familiar term symptoms even though dogs don't have symptoms, which are verbal descriptions of the patient's feelings: dogs have clinical signs. Since dogs can't speak, we have to look for clinical signs...but we still use the term symptoms in this book.

As a general rule, medicine is practised. That term is not arbitrary. Medicine is a constantly changing art as we learn more and more about genetics, electronic aids (like CAT scans) and daily laboratory advances. There are many dog maladies, like canine hip dysplasia, which are not universally treated in the same manner. Some veterinary surgeons opt for surgery more often than others do.

SELECTING A VETERINARY SURGEON

Your selection of a veterinary surgeon should not be based upon personality (as most are) but upon their convenience to your home. You want a doctor who is close because you might have emergencies or need to make multiple visits for treatments. You want a doctor who has services that you might require such as a boarding kennel and grooming facilities, as well as sophisticated pet supplies and a good reputation for ability and responsiveness. There is nothing more frustrating than having to wait a day or more to get a response from your veterinary surgeon.

All veterinary surgeons are licensed and their diplomas and/or certificates should be displayed in their waiting rooms. There are, however, many veterinary specialities that usually

Before you buy your Havanese, interview the veterinary surgeons in your area and select the one who best suits your needs. Discuss his schedule of fees, policies, and office and emergency hours.

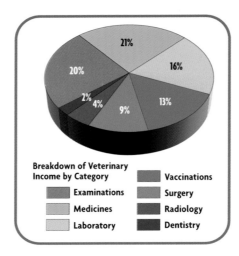

Breakdown of Veterinary Income by Category

- Examinations
- Medicines
- Laboratory
- Vaccinations
- Surgery
- Radiology
- Dentistry

require further studies and internships. There are specialists in heart problems (veterinary cardiologists), skin problems (veterinary dermatologists), teeth and gum problems (veterinary dentists), eye problems (veterinary ophthalmologists), X-rays (veterinary radiologists), and surgeons who have specialities in bones, muscles or other organs. Most veterinary surgeons do routine surgery such as neutering, stitching up wounds and docking tails for those breeds in which such is required for show purposes. When the problem affecting your dog is serious, it is not unusual or impudent to get another medical opinion, although in Britain you are obliged to advise the vets concerned about this. You might also want to compare costs amongst several veterinary surgeons. Sophisticated health care and vet-

erinary services can be very costly. Don't be bashful about discussing these costs with your veterinary surgeon or his (her) staff. It is not infrequent that important decisions are based upon financial considerations.

PREVENTATIVE MEDICINE

It is much easier, less costly and more effective to practise preventative medicine than to fight bouts of illness and disease. Properly bred puppies come from parents that were selected based upon their genetic disease profile. Their mothers should have been vaccinated, free of all internal and external parasites, and properly nourished. For these reasons, a visit to the veterinary surgeon who cared for the dam (mother) is recommended. The dam can pass on disease resistance to her puppies, which can last for eight to ten weeks. She can also pass on parasites and many infections. That's why you should visit the veterinary surgeon who cared for the dam.

WEANING TO FIVE MONTHS OLD

Puppies should be weaned by the time they are about two months old. A puppy that remains for at least eight weeks with its mother and litter mates usually adapts better to other dogs and people later in its life.

Some new owners have their puppy examined by a veterinary

First Aid
at a Glance

Burns
Place the affected area under cool water; use ice if only a small area is burnt.

Bee/Insect bites
Apply ice to relieve swelling; antihistamine dosed properly.

Animal bites
Clean any bleeding area; apply pressure until bleeding subsides; go to the vet.

Spider bites
Use cold compress and a pressurised pack to inhibit venom's spreading.

Antifreeze poisoning
Immediately induce vomiting by using hydrogen peroxide.

Fish hooks
Removal best handled by vet; hook must be cut in order to remove.

Snake bites
Pack ice around bite; contact vet quickly; identify snake for proper antivenin.

Car accident
Move dog from roadway with blanket; seek veterinary aid.

Shock
Calm the dog, keep him warm; seek immediate veterinary help.

Nosebleed
Apply cold compress to the nose; apply pressure to any visible abrasion.

Bleeding
Apply pressure above the area; treat wound by applying a cotton pack.

Heat stroke
Submerge dog in cold bath; cool down with fresh air and water; go to the vet.

Frostbite/Hypothermia
Warm the dog with a warm bath, electric blankets or hot water bottles.

Abrasions
Clean the wound and wash out thoroughly with fresh water; apply antiseptic.

Remember: an injured dog may attempt to bite a helping hand from fear and confusion. Always muzzle the dog before trying to offer assistance.

surgeon immediately, which is a good idea. Vaccination programmes usually begin when the puppy is very young.

The puppy will have its teeth examined and have its skeletal conformation and general health checked prior to certification by the veterinary surgeon. Puppies in certain breeds have problems with their kneecaps, eye cataracts and other eye problems, heart murmurs and undescended testicles. They may also have personality problems and your veterinary surgeon might have training in temperament evaluation.

VACCINATION SCHEDULING

Most vaccinations are given by injection and should only be done by a veterinary surgeon. Both he and you should keep a record of the date of the

DID YOU KNOW?

Caring for the puppy starts before the puppy is born by keeping the dam healthy and well-nourished. Most puppies have worms, even if they are not evident, so a worming programme is essential. The worms continually shed eggs except during their dormant stage, when they just rest in the tissues of the puppy. During this stage they are not evident during a routine examination.

injection, the identification of the vaccine and the amount given. Some vets give a first vaccination at eight weeks, but most dog breeders prefer the course not to commence until about ten weeks because of negating any antibodies passed on by the dam. The vaccination scheduling is usually based on a 15-day cycle. You must take your vet's advice as to when to vaccinate as this may differ according to the vaccine used. Most vaccinations immunise your puppy against viruses.

The usual vaccines contain immunising doses of several different viruses such as distemper, parvovirus, parainfluenza and hepatitis. There are other vaccines available when the puppy is at risk. You should rely upon professional advice. This is especially true for the booster-shot programme. Most vaccination programmes require a booster when the puppy is a year old and once a year thereafter. In some cases, circumstances may require more frequent immunisations.

The most serious diseases that affect the Havanese also affect any other dog: parvovirus, adenovirus, coronavirus, distemper, hepatitis, leptospirosis, and rabies. All these diseases are fatal in more than 90 percent of cases. The only sure way to prevent them is to vaccinate your dog. Always ask the breeder for worming and vaccination certificates in addition to the pedigree.

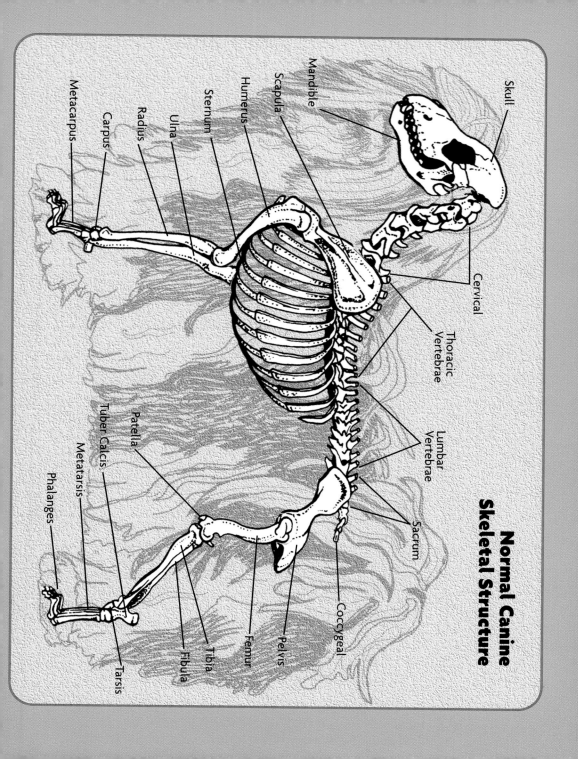

Normal Canine
Skeletal Structure

Skull
Cervical
Mandible
Scapula
Sternum
Humerus
Thoracic Vertebrae
Radius
Ulna
Carpus
Metacarpus
Lumbar Vertebrae
Sacrum
Coccygeal
Pelvis
Femur
Tibia
Fibula
Patella
Tuber Calcis
Metatarsis
Tarsis
Phalanges

HEALTH AND VACCINATION SCHEDULE

AGE IN WEEKS:	3RD	6TH	8TH	10TH	12TH	14TH	16TH	20-24TH
Worm Control	✔	✔	✔	✔	✔	✔	✔	✔
Neutering								✔
Heartworm*		✔						✔
Parvovirus		✔		✔		✔		✔
Distemper			✔		✔		✔	
Hepatitis			✔		✔		✔	
Leptospirosis		✔		✔		✔		
Parainfluenza		✔		✔		✔		
Dental Examination			✔					✔
Complete Physical			✔					✔
Temperament Testing			✔					
Coronavirus					✔			
Canine Cough		✔						
Hip Dysplasia							✔	
Rabies*								✔

Vaccinations are not instantly effective. It takes about two weeks for the dog's immunisation system to develop antibodies. Most vaccinations require annual booster shots. Your veterinary surgeon should guide you in this regard.
*Not applicable in the United Kingdom

Kennel cough, more formally known as tracheobronchitis, is treated with a vaccine that is sprayed into the dog's nostrils. Kennel cough is usually included in routine vaccination, but this is often not so effective as for other major diseases.

FIVE MONTHS TO ONE YEAR OF AGE
Unless you intend to breed or show your dog, neutering the puppy at six months of age is recommended. Discuss this with your veterinary surgeon.

By the time your Bichon Havanese is seven or eight months of age, he can be seriously evaluated for his conformation to the standard, thus determining show potential and desirability as a sire or dam. If the puppy is not top class and therefore is not a candi-

DID YOU KNOW?
Not every dog's ears are the same. Ears that are open to the air are healthier than ears with poor air circulation. Sometimes a dog can have two differently shaped ears. You should not probe inside your dog's ears. Only clean that which is accessible with a wad of soft cotton wool.

date for a serious breeding programme, most professionals
advise neutering the puppy.
Neutering has proven to be
extremely beneficial to both male
and female puppies. Besides
eliminating the possibility of
pregnancy, it inhibits (but does
not prevent) breast cancer in
bitches and prostate cancer in
male dogs. Under no circumstances should a bitch be spayed
prior to her first season.

DOGS OLDER THAN ONE YEAR
Continue to visit the veterinary
surgeon at least once a year. There
is no such disease as old age, but
bodily functions do change with

DID YOU KNOW?
Vaccines do not work all the time.
Sometimes dogs are allergic to them
and many times the antibodies, which
are supposed to be stimulated by the
vaccine, just are not produced. You
should keep your dog in the veterinary
clinic for an hour after it is vaccinated to
be sure there are no allergic reactions.

age. The eyes and ears are no
longer as efficient. Liver, kidney
and intestinal functions often
decline. Proper dietary changes,
recommended by your veterinary
surgeon, can make life more
pleasant for the ageing Bichon
Havanese and you.

Disease	What is it?	What causes it?	Symptoms
Leptospirosis	Severe disease that affects the internal organs; can be spread to people.	A bacterium, which is often carried by rodents, that enters through mucous membranes and spreads quickly throughout the body.	Range from fever, vomiting and loss of appetite in less severe cases to shock, irreversible kidney damage and possibly death in most severe cases.
Rabies	Potentially deadly virus that infects warm-blooded mammals. Not seen in United Kingdom.	Bite from a carrier of the virus, mainly wild animals.	1st stage: dog exhibits change in behaviour, fear. 2nd stage: dog's behaviour becomes more aggressive. 3rd stage: loss of coordination, trouble with bodily functions.
Parvovirus	Highly contagious virus, potentially deadly.	Ingestion of the virus, which is usually spread through the faeces of infected dogs.	Most common: severe diarrhoea. Also vomiting, fatigue, lack of appetite.
Kennel cough	Contagious respiratory infection.	Combination of types of bacteria and virus. Most common: *Bordetella bronchiseptica* bacteria and parainfluenza virus.	Chronic cough.
Distemper	Disease primarily affecting respiratory and nervous system.	Virus that is related to the human measles virus.	Mild symptoms such as fever, lack of appetite and mucous secretion progress to evidence of brain damage, 'hard pad.'
Hepatitis	Virus primarily affecting the liver.	Canine adenovirus type I (CAV-1). Enters system when dog breathes in particles.	Lesser symptoms include listlessness, diarrhoea, vomiting. More severe symptoms include 'blue-eye' (clumps of virus in eye).
Coronavirus	Virus resulting in digestive problems.	Virus is spread through infected dog's faeces.	Stomach upset evidenced by lack of appetite, vomiting, diarrhoea.

Other less serious health problems in adult dogs include eye and ear infections that can occur if you neglect cleaning the eyes and are careless about water entering the ears during bathing. A good way of detecting ear problems is to smell his ears, since any strange odour may indicate that something's wrong. Another method is to place your own ear next to your dog's whilst you rub the outside of his ear where it joins the head. If the ear has accumulated water or any other liquid, you will easily hear it moving inside the ear.

Skin irritations are another problem and some Havaneses are accustomed to biting their skin in certain areas. The saliva thus accumulated moistens that part of the skin and causes the hair to stick to it, which may cause a small epidermal eruption that can easily be treated by shaving the irritated area and applying the indicated medicine.

DID YOU KNOW?
Your veterinary surgeon will probably recommend that your puppy be vaccinated before you take him outside. There are airborne diseases, parasite eggs in the grass and unexpected visits from other dogs that might be dangerous to your puppy's health.

The routine of going over your pet at least once a week is very useful, for it permits you to detect any problem before it becomes serious. Remember that he can't talk, that he will tolerate considerable pain and that, as an animal, he tends to be more stoic and uncomplaining about his problems than we humans are.

Check his mouth to make sure there are no residues that could cause future gum problems. Check between the toes and pads of the feet to find any hard little objects that may become lodged there.

Dogs occasionally have diarrhoea when the diet is changed, when they overeat or when they drink too much milk, especially if they aren't accustomed to it. This is normal. But never overlook diarrhoea. Many diseases can begin with an apparently insignificant case of diarrhoea. However, if your dog is properly vaccinated, there's a large measure of security that he won't suffer from any of them.

SKIN PROBLEMS IN BICHONS HAVANESES

Veterinary surgeons are consulted by dog owners for skin problems more than any other group of diseases or maladies. Dogs' skin is almost as sensitive as human skin and both suffer almost the same ailments. (Though the occurrence of acne in dogs is rare!) For this reason, veterinary dermatology has developed into a speciality practised by many veterinary surgeons.

Since many skin problems have visual symptoms that are almost identical, it requires the skill of an experienced veterinary dermatologist to identify and cure many of the more severe skin disorders. Pet shops sell many treatments for skin problems but most of the treatments are directed at symptoms and not the underlying problem(s). If your dog is suffering from a skin disorder, you should seek professional assistance as quickly as possible. As with all diseases, the earlier a problem is identified and treated, the more successful is the cure.

AUTO-IMMUNE SKIN CONDITIONS
Auto-immune skin conditions are commonly referred to as being allergic to yourself, whilst allergies are usually inflammatory reactions to an outside stimulus. Auto-immune diseases cause serious damage to the tissues that are involved.

The best known auto-immune disease is lupus, which affects people as well as dogs. The symptoms are variable and may affect the kidneys, bones, blood chemistry and skin. It can be fatal to both dogs and humans, though it is not thought to be transmissible. It is usually successfully treated with cortisone, prednisone or similar corticosteroid, but extensive

DID YOU KNOW?
There is a 4:1 chance of a puppy getting this fatal gene combination from two parents with recessive genes for acrodermatitis:

AA= NORMAL, HEALTHY
aa= FATAL
Aa= RECESSIVE, NORMAL APPEARING

If the female parent has an Aa gene and the male parent has an Aa gene, the chances are one in four that the puppy will have the fatal genetic combination aa.

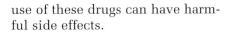

Dam ♀

		A	a
Sire ♂	A	AA	Aa
	a	Aa	aa

use of these drugs can have harmful side effects.

INHERITED SKIN PROBLEMS
Many skin disorders are inherited and some are fatal. For example, Acrodermatitis is an inherited disease that is transmitted by both parents. The parents, who appear (phenotypically) normal, have a recessive gene for acrodermatitis, meaning that they carry, but are not affected by the disease.

Acrodermatitis is just one example of how difficult it is to

131

prevent congenital dog diseases. The cost and skills required to ascertain whether two dogs should be mated are too high even though puppies with acrodermatitis rarely reach two years of age.

Other inherited skin problems are usually not as fatal as acrodermatitis. All inherited diseases must be diagnosed and treated by a veterinary specialist. There are active programmes being undertaken by many veterinary pharmaceutical manufacturers to solve most, if not all, of the common skin problems of dogs.

PARASITE BITES
Many of us are allergic to insect bites. The bites itch, erupt and may even become infected. Dogs have the same reaction to fleas, ticks and/or mites. When an insect lands on you, you have the chance to whisk it away with your hand. Unfortunately, when our dog is bitten by a flea, tick or mite, it can only scratch it away or bite it. By the time the dog has been bitten, the

DID YOU KNOW?
The myth that dogs need extra fat in their diets can be harmful. Should your vet recommend extra fat, use safflower oil instead of animal oils. Safflower oil has been shown to be less likely to cause allergic reactions.

parasite has done some of its damage. It may also have laid eggs to cause further problems in the near future. The itching from parasite bites is probably due to the saliva injected into the site when the parasite sucks the dog's blood.

AIRBORNE ALLERGIES
Another interesting allergy is pollen allergy. Humans have hay fever, rose fever and other fevers with which they suffer during the pollinating season. Many dogs suffer the same allergies. When the pollen count is high, your dog might suffer but don't expect them to sneeze and have runny noses like humans. Dogs react to pollen allergies the same way they react to fleas—they scratch and bite themselves.

Dogs, like humans, can be tested for allergens. Discuss the testing with your veterinary dermatologist.

FOOD ALLERGIES
Dogs are allergic to many foods that are best-sellers and highly recommended by breeders and veterinary surgeons. Changing the brand of food that you buy may not eliminate the problem if the element to which the dog is allergic is contained in the new brand.

Recognising a food allergy is difficult. Humans vomit or have rashes when they eat a food to which they are allergic. Dogs neither vomit nor (usually) develop a

DID YOU KNOW?
Feeding your dog properly is very important. An incorrect diet could affect the dog's health, behaviour and nervous system, possibly making a normal dog into an aggressive one.

rash. They react in the same manner as they do to an airborne or flea allergy: they itch, scratch and bite. Thus making the diagnosis extremely difficult. Whilst pollen allergies and parasite bites are usually seasonal, food allergies are year-round problems.

FOOD INTOLERANCE
Food intolerance is the inability of the dog to completely digest certain foods. Puppies that may have done very well on their mother's milk may not do well on cow's milk. The rest of this food intolerance may be lose bowels, passing gas and stomach pains. These are the only obvious symptoms of food intolerance and that makes diagnosis difficult.

TREATING FOOD PROBLEMS
It is possible to handle food allergies and food intolerance yourself. Put your dog on a diet that it has never had. Obviously if it has never eaten this new food it can't have been allergic or intolerant of it. Start with a single ingredient that is not in the dog's diet at the present time. Ingredients like

chopped beef or fish are common in dog's diets, so try something more exotic like rabbit, pheasant or even just vegetables. Keep the dog on this diet (with no additives) for a month. If the symptoms of food allergy or intolerance disappear, chances are your dog has a food allergy.

Don't think that the single ingredient cured the problem. You still must find a suitable diet and ascertain which ingredient in the old diet was objectionable. This is most easily done by adding ingredients to the new diet one at a time. Let the dog stay on the modified diet for a month before you add another ingredient. Eventually, you will determine the ingredient that caused the adverse reaction.

An alternative method is to carefully study the ingredients in the diet to which your dog is allergic or intolerable. Identify the main ingredient in this diet and eliminate the main ingredient by buying a different food that does not have that ingredient. Keep experimenting until the symptoms disappear after one month on the new diet.

GENETIC DISEASES OF THE HAVANESE
Thanks to the advances of science and technology, it is now possible to identify a series of diseases of genetic origin in dogs. This imposes an important responsibility on

breeders, who have to be aware of and make every effort to eradicate the diseases that can affect the animals they breed. Almost every breed is subject to one or more.

Ask the breeder or owner from whom you acquire your dog to give you some certification that the pup's parents and grandparents are healthy specimens; otherwise you run the risk of having an animal that will give you only headaches instead of joy.

It's also advisable to take your newly acquired pup to a veterinarian for a complete examination. If any defects show up, you can then decide whether to return the dog or keep it. An animal with genetic defects or diseases should never be used for breeding.

Amongst the diseases of genetic origin in the Bichon Havanese are cataracts and PRA (progressive retina atrophy), which usually causes blindness in the afflicted animal. They have been detected in Havaneses bred in the United States and in some European countries.

The only way to detect PRA is through a special test, although the dog often presents symptoms such as increased size of the pupil, limited vision and even blindness. This disease is very hard to eradicate, since it often occurs in adult-

hood, when the diagnosis is too late to prevent reproduction. Nevertheless, because of its recurrence in the United States, according to Havanese breeders there, it is of vital importance to examine the entire litter early on, and then check each dog annually to make sure the problem doesn't exist.

Complicating the eradication of PRA is the fact that the gene responsible for producing it is a recessive gene, so the dog can be a carrier without actually having the disease. If a carrier is bred with a healthy animal, the offspring will be healthy, but 50 percent will be carriers. When two apparently healthy carriers are bred, the situation is further complicated as 50 percent of the litter will be carriers and 25 percent will be diseased. In an even worse case, that of breeding a healthy dog with a diseased dog, the result will be that 100 percent of the litter will be carriers although they appear to be healthy.

These numbers may sound a bit schematic, but they give us an idea of how important it is to pay attention to this problem. Once the recessive gene for PRA has entered the breeding line, it will be passed from generation to generation until another recessive gene for PRA is encountered. Only then will the disease appear as proof that the line was actually affected.

EXTERNAL PARASITES

Of all the problems to which dogs are prone, none is more well known and frustrating than fleas. Fleas, which usually refers to fleas, ticks and mites, are difficult to prevent but relatively simple to cure. Parasites that are harboured inside the body are more difficult to cure but they are easier to control. These ectoparasites lodge themselves on the upper part of the dog's body, in the coat and on the skin, causing such ailments as itching, baldness and skin lesions due to scratching.

FLEAS

To control a flea infestation you have to understand the life cycle of a typical flea. Fleas are often thought of as a summertime problem but centrally heated homes have rather changed the pattern and fleas can be found at any time of the year. There is no single flea-control medicine (insecticide) that can be used in every flea-infested area. To understand flea control you must apply suitable treatment to the weak link in the life cycle of the flea.

THE LIFE CYCLE OF A FLEA

Fleas are found in four forms: eggs, larvae, pupae and adults. You really need a low-power microscope or hand lens to identify a living flea's eggs, pupae or larva. They spend their whole lives on your Bichon Havanese unless they are forcibly removed by brushing, bathing, scratching or biting.

The dog flea is scientifically known as *Ctenocephalides canis* whilst the cat flea is *Ctenocephalides felis*. Several species infest both dog and cats.

Fleas lay eggs whilst they are in residence upon your dog. These eggs fall off almost as soon as they dry (they may be a bit damp when initially

A scanning electron micrograph of a dog flea, *Ctenocephalides canis*.
S.E.M. by Dr. Dennis Kunkel, University of Hawaii.

DID YOU KNOW?

Flea-killers are poisonous. You should not spray these toxic chemicals on areas of the dog's body that he licks, on his genitals or on his face. Flea-killers taken internally are a better answer, but check with your vet in case internal therapy is not advised for your dog.

135

laid) and are the reservoir of future flea infestations. If your dog scratches himself and is able to dislodge a few fleas, they simply fall off and await a future chance to attack a dog...or even a person. Yes, fleas from dogs bite people. That's why it is so important to control fleas both on the dog and in the dog's entire environment. You must, therefore, treat the dog and the environment simultaneously.

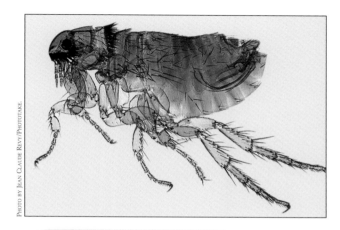

PHOTO BY JEAN CLAUDE RÉVY/PHOTOTAKE.

A scanning electron micrograph of a dog flea, *Ctenocephalides canis.*

DE-FLEAING THE HOME

Cleanliness is the simple rule. If you have a cat living with your dog, the matter is more complicated since most dog fleas are actually cat fleas. Cats climb onto many areas that are never accessible to dogs (like window sills, table tops, etc.), so you have to clean all of these areas. The hard floor surfaces (tiles, wood, stone and linoleum) must be mopped several times a day. Drops of food onto the floor are actually food for flea larvae! All rugs and furniture must be vacuumed several times a day. Don't forget cupboards, under furniture and cushions. A study has reported that a vacuum cleaner with a beater bar can remove only 20% of the larvae and 50% of the eggs. The vacuum bags should be discarded into a sealed plastic bag or burned. The vacuum machine itself should be cleaned. The outdoor area to which your dog has access must also be treated with an insecticide.

DID YOU KNOW?

Ivermectin is quickly becoming the drug of choice for treating many parasitic skin diseases in dogs.

For some unknown reason, herding dogs like Collies, Old English Sheepdogs and German Shepherds, etc., are extremely sensitive to ivermectin.

Ivermectin injections have killed some dogs, but dogs heavily infected with skin disorders may be treated anyway.

The ivermectin reaction is a toxicosis which causes tremors, loss of power to move their muscles, prolonged dilatation of the pupil of the eye, coma (unconsciousness), or cessation of breathing (death).

The toxicosis usually starts from 4-6 hours after ingestion or as late as 12 hours. The longer it takes to set in, the milder is the reaction.

Ivermectin should only be prescribed and administered by a vet. Some ivermectin treatments require two doses.

(FACING PAGE) S.E.M. of a dog or cat flea, *Ctenocephalides* magnified more than 100 times its actual size. It has been colourised for effect. S.E.M. by Dr. Dennis Kunkel, University of Hawaii.

137

Your vet will be able to recommend a household insecticidal spray, but this must be used with caution and instructions strictly adhered to.

Male cat fleas, *Ctenocephalides felis*, are very commonly found on dogs.

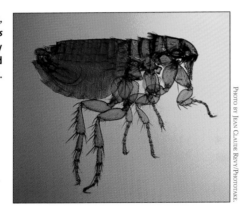

Photo by Jean Claude Révy/Phototake.

There are many drugs available to kill fleas on the dog itself, such as the miracle drug ivermectin, and it is best to have the de-fleaing and de-worming supervised by your vet. Ivermectin is effective against many external and internal parasites including heartworms, roundworms, tapeworms, flukes, ticks and mites. It has not been approved for use to control these pests, but veterinary surgeons frequently use it anyway. Ivermectin may not be available in all areas.

Dwight R. Kuhn's magnificent action photo showing a flea jumping from a dog's back.

Sterilising the Environment
Besides cleaning your home with vacuum cleaners and mops, you have to treat the outdoor range of your dog. When trimming bushes and spreading insecticide, be careful not to poison areas in which fishes or other animals reside.

Ticks and Mites
Though not as common as fleas, ticks and mites are found all over the tropical and temperate world. They don't bite like fleas, they harpoon. They dig their sharp proboscis (nose) into the dog's skin and drink the blood, which is their only food and drink. Dogs can get paralysis, Lyme disease, Rocky Mountain spotted fever (normally found in the U.S. only), and many other diseases from ticks and mites. They may live where fleas are found but they also like to hide in cracks or seams in walls wherever dogs live. They are controlled the same way fleas are controlled.

Vegetal parasites, which accompany a lack of hygiene,

Photo by Dwight R. Kuhn.

The Life Cycle of the Flea

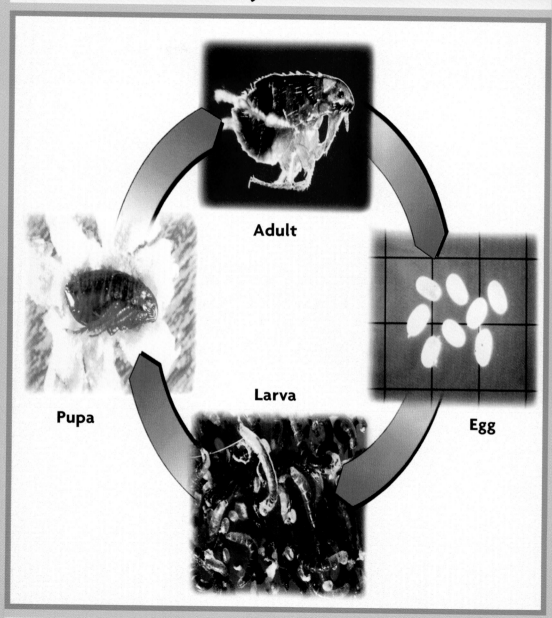

Adult

Egg

Larva

Pupa

The Life Cycle of the Flea was posterised by Fleabusters® Rx for Fleas,
to whom we are indebted for allowing us to reproduce it here.

The eggs of the dog flea.

also affect the dog in the form of trichomonads and other fungi that produce circular bald spots on the body and sometimes infect the ears.

The tick *Dermacentor variabilis* may well be the most common dog tick in many geographical areas, especially where the climate is hot and humid.

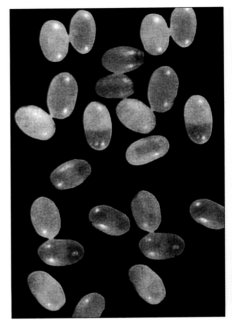

DID YOU KNOW?

There are drugs which prevent fleas from maturing from egg to adult.

The weak link is the maturation from a larva to a pupa.

Methoprene and fenoxycarb mimic the effect of maturation enhancers, thus, in effect, killing the larva before it pupates.

Methoprene is mildly effective in killing flea eggs while fenoxycarb is better able to stand UV rays from the sun. There is a combination of both drugs which has an effective life of 6 months and destroys 93% of the flea population.

There are desiccants which dry out the eggs, larvae and adult fleas. These desiccants are common, well known and do not usually affect dogs, cats, humans or other mammalian animals.

Desiccants include silica gel, sodium borate and diatomaceous earth. The best known and most effective is polymerized borate which is marketed by Rx for Fleas Plus® (Fleabusters®).

Most dog ticks have life expectancies of a week to six months, depending upon climatic conditions. They neither jump nor fly, but crawl slowly and can range up to 5 metres (16 feet) to reach a sleeping or unsuspecting dog.

MANGE

Microscopic mites are among the dangerous animal parasites, especially the *Sarcoptes* that burrow into the skin of the head and face, producing sarcoptic mange; and the *Demodex* that provoke demodetic mange and are very difficult to cure.

Mange is a skin irritation caused by mites. Some mites are contagious, like

Cheyletiella, ear mites, scabies and chiggers. The non-contagious mites are *Demodex*. The most serious of the mites is the one that causes ear-mite infestation. Ear mites are usually controlled with ivermectin.

It is essential that your dog be treated for mange as quickly as possible because some forms of mange are transmissible to people.

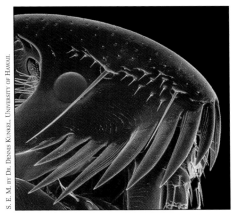

Magnified head of a dog flea, *Ctenocephalides canis.*

S. E. M. BY DR. DENNIS KUNKEL, UNIVERSITY OF HAWAII.

you encounter an infestation of ectoparasites, don't forget to disinfect the areas where your dog spends his time, where he sleeps, where he plays, etc.

A brown dog tick, *Rhipicephalus sanguineus*, is an uncommon but annoying tick found on dogs.

INTERNAL PARASITES
Most animals—fishes, birds and mammals, including dogs and

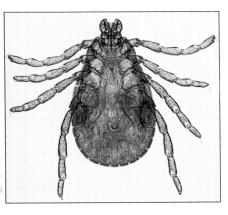

An infinite number of products are available to eliminate external parasites. They should be applied according to directions, but you should remain alert. By systematically checking your dog as we have suggested, you will be able to counteract any ectoparasite at once. Some owners complain that, in spite of regular worming, their dogs still have parasites. And the reason is very simple. As we have said, parasites inhabit the animal and the environment, so if

Human lice look like dog lice; the two are closely related.

PHOTO BY DWIGHT R. KUHN

141

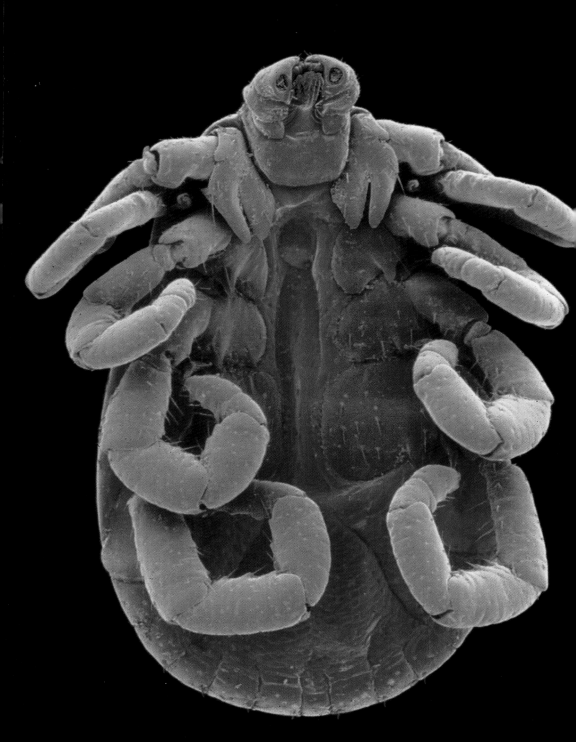

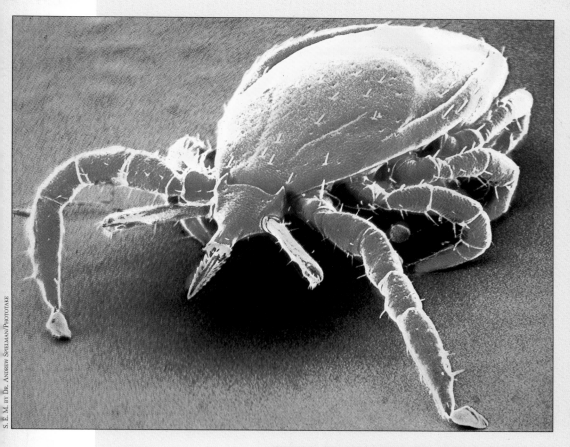

(ABOVE)
The deer tick that carries Lyme disease.

(RIGHT)
The dog tick of the genus *Ixode.*

(FACING PAGE)
The dog tick, *Dermacentor variabilis,* is probably the most common tick found on dogs. Imagine the holdfast strength in its eight legs! No wonder it is hard to detach them!

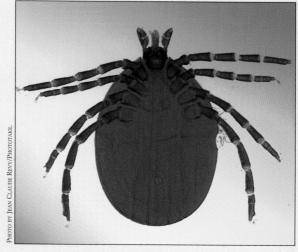

Magnified view of
the mange mite,
Psoroptes bovis.

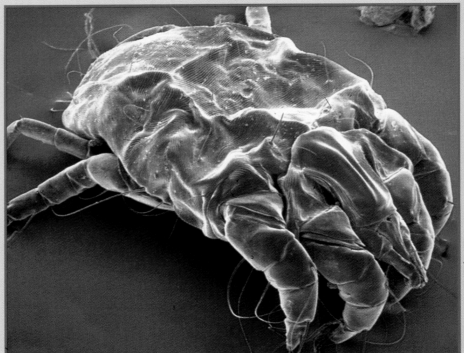

S. E. M. BY DR. DENNIS KUNKEL, UNIVERSITY OF HAWAII.

Internal parasites are numerous; they come round and flat, in diverse forms and sizes. Amongst the most common are: *Toxocara canis, Toxocara leonina, Dipylidium caninum, Trichuris vulpis, Dirofilaria inmitis* (transmitted by a mosquito), intestinal worms, tapeworms and hookworms. All of them cause a variety of infirmities. Some can easily be observed in canine faeces, but others can only be detected through laboratory analysis of the faeces. One of the most common symptoms is diarrhoea, but bloody or viscous faeces are also suspicious. Some parasites are transmitted from the pregnant bitch to her litter. That is why, as we have indicated, puppies receive a regular series of routine wormings, which should continue on a regular basis. If the dog lives alone, in a healthy environment and seldom goes outdoors, a general annual worming may be sufficient. However, if he lives with other dogs or animals, goes outside frequently, travels with his owner, or leads an active life in dog shows where he is in contact with other dogs and other environments, the dog should be wormed more frequently, perhaps every three

The head of the dog tick, *Dermacentor variabilis.*

humans—have worms and other parasites that live inside their bodies. According to Dr. Herbert R. Axelrod, the fish pathologist, there are two kinds of parasites: dumb and smart. The smart parasites live in peaceful cooperation with their hosts (symbiosis), whilst the dumb parasites kill their host. Most of the worm infections are relatively easy to control. If they are not controlled they eventually weaken the host dog to the point that other medical problems occur, but they are not dumb parasites that directly cause the death of their hosts.

145

The roundworm can infect both dogs and humans.

PHOTO BY CAROLINA BIOLOGICAL SUPPLY/PHOTOTAKE.

The heart of a dog infected with canine heart-worm, *Dirofilaria immitis.*

PHOTO BY JAMES E. HAYDEN, RPB/PHOTOTAKE.

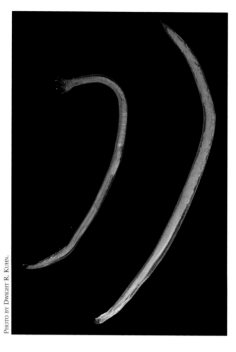

PHOTO BY DWIGHT R. KUHN.

Male and female hookworms, *Ancylostoma caninum*, are uncommonly found in pet or show dogs in Britain. Hookworms may infect other dogs that have exposure to grasslands

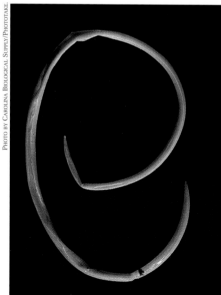

PHOTO BY CAROLINA BIOLOGICAL SUPPLY/PHOTOTAKE.

The roundworm *Rhabditis*.

months. For specific guidance, con-sult your veterinarian.

A recommendable measure for arresting parasitic reinfection is to dispose of your dog's faeces during the worming process so he has no further contact with the discharge.

ROUNDWORMS

The roundworms that infect dogs are scientifically known as *Toxocara canis*. They live in the dog's intestine and shed eggs con-tinually. It has been estimated that an average-sized dog produces about 150 grammes of faeces every day. Each gramme of faeces averages 10,000–12,000 eggs of roundworms. All areas in which dogs roam contain astronomical numbers of roundworm eggs. The greatest danger of roundworms is that they infect people, too! It is wise to have your dog tested regularly for roundworms.

Pigs also have roundworm infections that can be passed to human and dogs. The typical pig roundworm parasite is called *Ascaris lumbricoides.*

HOOKWORMS

The worm *Ancylostoma caninum* is commonly called the dog hookworm. It is also dangerous to humans and cats. It attaches itself to the dog's intestines by its teeth. It changes the site of its attachment about six times a day, and the dog loses blood from each detachment. This blood loss can cause iron-deficiency anaemia. Hookworms are easily purged from the dog with many medications, the best of which seems to be ivermectin even though it has not been approved for such use.

In Britain, the 'temperate climate' hookworm (*Uncinaria stenocephala*) is rarely found in pet or show dogs, but can occur in hunting packs, racing Greyhounds and sheepdogs because these hookworms can be prevalent wherever dogs are exercised regularly on grassland.

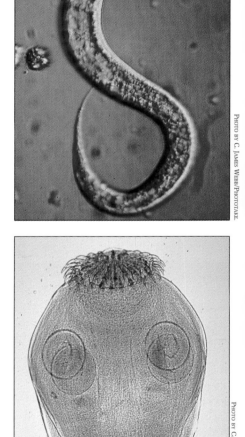

TAPEWORMS

There are many species of tapeworms, many of which are carried by fleas! The dog eats the flea and starts the tapeworm cycle. Humans can also be infected with tapeworms, so don't eat fleas! Fleas are so small that your dog could pass them onto your hands, your plate or your food and make it possible for you to ingest a flea which is carrying tapeworm eggs.

Whilst tapeworm infection is not life threatening in dogs (smart parasite!), it can be the cause of a very serious liver disease for humans. About 50 percent of the humans infected with *Echinococcus multilocularis*, causing alveolar hydatis, perish.

HEARTWORMS

Heartworms are thin, extended worms up to 30 cms. (12 ins.) long that live in a dog's heart and the major blood vessels around it. Bichons Havaneses may have up to 200 of these worms. The symptoms may be loss of energy, loss of appetite, coughing, the development of a pot belly and anaemia.

Heartworms are transmitted by mosquitoes. The mosquito drinks the blood of an infected dog and takes in larvae with the blood. The larvae, called microfilaria, develop within the body of the mosquito and are passed on to the next dog bitten after the larvae mature. It takes two to three weeks for the larvae to develop to the infective stage within the body of the mosquito. Dogs should be treated at about six weeks of age, then every six months.

Blood testing for heartworms is not necessarily indicative of how seriously your dog is infected. This is a dangerous disease. Although heartworm affects dogs in the United States, Asia, Australia, and Central Europe, dogs in Britain are not affected by heartworm.

DID YOU KNOW?
There are many parasiticides which can be used around your home and garden to control fleas.

Natural pyrethrins can be used inside the house.

Allethrin, bioallethrin, permethrin and resmethrin can also be used inside the house but permethrin has been used successfully outdoors, too.

Carbaryl can be used indoors and outdoors.

Propoxur can be used indoors.

Chlorpyrifos, diazinon and malathion can be used indoors or outdoors and it has an extended residual activity.

SHOWING YOUR
Bichon Havanese

INITIAL CONSIDERATIONS

If you want your Havanese to compete in dog shows, here are a few things you should know.

First, your Havanese must know how to trot in a straight line, on leash, at his owner's left side. He must be able to stop on command and remain quiet whilst the judge does a physical examination that includes the mouth and, in the case of a male, the testicles. At all times, the dog should maintain the correct posture: head and neck held high and an alert disposition, whether moving or standing still.posture

Since small breeds are examined on a table, it is useful for you to teach your pup how to pose on an elevated surface, by holding up his head with your left hand and his tail with your right hand. Give him a command such as 'Stay' and try to maintain this position for a few seconds and, in time, for two or three minutes. Every time he obeys you, caress him, praise him, let him know he's doing just what you asked him to do. For that reason, your dog must not identify the table with a

Ambar, Champion of Champions, owned by Barbara Monteagudo and shared by Merita Batista and Zoila Portuondo, is showing off his ribbons. What could make a loving Havanese owner more happy than having his dog selected by the judge!

disagreeable experience, such as being injected or having his nails cut (no dog enjoys having its nails trimmed), so find some place else to perform these tasks. Otherwise, he may resist when

you try to pose him on the table during the show.

To make your dog gait correctly, you must first make sure that his collar is placed high on the neck just behind the ears so he won't lower his head. If you use a choke collar, make sure the slip is always on top so you can control your Havanese from the other end of the leash, relaxing or applying the pressure of the collar on the dog's neck. Round leather check collars are generally used for training and a different type of collar, made of fine cord, is used in the show ring. Do not use a chain link collar on a Havanese as it can damage the dog's silky coat.

The correct way to pose a dog is as follows: maintain the head

A judge in Havana examining the Havanese on the table. As with other toy breeds, the handler must place the dog on the table for the judge to examine its structure.

DID YOU KNOW?

You can get information about dog shows from kennel clubs and breed clubs:

Fédération Cynologique Internationale
14, rue Leopold II, B-6530 Thuin, Belgium

The Kennel Club
1-5 Clarges Street
Piccadilly, London W1Y 8AB, UK
www.the-kennel-club.org.uk

American Kennel Club
5580 Centerview Drive
Raleigh, NC 27606-3390, USA
www.akc.org

Canadian Kennel Club
89 Skyway Ave., Suite 100, Etobicoke,
Ontario M9W 6R4 Canada
www.ckc.ca

The Havanese breed standard indicates three bites that are faulty: overshot, undershot and clamped. The judge will examine the Havanese's bite to be certain it is the desirable scissors bite.

151

The Havanese should act confidently and calmly as the judge makes the physical examination. This dog show is underway in Havana.

high, holding it with the collar or the left hand. The front legs should be perpendicular to the ground (or the table), solidly planted and parallel to each other. To do this, hold first one and then the other front leg at the elbow, raising each and lowering it in the proper position. The hindquarters are placed so the tarsal joints are completely perpendicular to the ground. This is accomplished by standing behind the dog whilst holding the leash with the left hand and raising first one and then the other rear paw to tarsus level. With your free hand, hold the tail up high.

At the Europasieger Show, Sandra's Fantastic Mr Florence, owned by Enka Fassott, has placed first in the group.

Training sessions for shows should be given daily for 10 to 15 minutes twice a day. Don't let your dog become bored, since he should present a happy disposition at show time and not look as if he's performing a tedious duty. My advice is to give him five min-

utes of freedom before and after each session, so he can run happily around the park and learn that a training session can also be fun.

Finally, before taking your Havanese to a show, attend one as a spectator. There you will watch experienced handlers and trained dogs at work. Ask questions; learn from them. Before you train your dog, you need to be trained to know exactly what to do and how to do it. You should know how to move in the ring, what steps to take so your Havanese trots properly, how to place him on the table, how to pose him, etc.

LIFE AS A SHOW DOG

There's still more to keep in mind if you plan to show your dog.

A show dog has to be protected and cared for all the time. You can't allow him to go digging in the garden, rooting around the plants in the park or playing with puppies, because

all of this can damage his coat. By this I don't mean you should make your dog a prisoner, as some handlers do. That would be abusive and harmful to his physical and temperamental health. However, it's obvious that you have to take different precautions with a show dog than you take with a family pet.

During the time you plan to present your dog in shows, try to have a professional groomer take care of his coat.

The show dog should also be perfectly socialised, since he has to share the ring with other dogs that he can neither attack nor fear. To ensure such behaviour, he should be exposed to other dogs in his training, of course only once his vaccinations are complete.

It is also good for him to have enough exercise so he's in top shape physically and, therefore, won't pant or tire easily. This will naturally have a positive influence on the way your Havanese walks and trots in the ring.

Accustom your show dog to spend two or three hours at a time inside his crate, because that's where he will have to wait his turn to enter the ring at the dog show. For show dogs, it's even more important that crate training is successful.

Remember that, before going to the show grounds, your Havanese must be bathed and carefully combed (don't divide the hair with the comb). Once you've found your waiting place on the show grounds, comb and brush him by hand for the final touch before he enters the ring. Always take a bottle of water and softener with you so you can dampen the coat slightly to make it even more beautiful.

Whilst awaiting your turn, keep your dog quiet inside his crate. Never permit him to run around the grounds. Better to take advantage of whatever time you have to brush his coat and check him over to make sure your Havanese is impeccable when he meets the judge.

Many hours of practising your Havanese's heeling and gaiting will be rewarded when your dog moves like a pro around the ring.

Competition in the puppy classes is usually less intense than in the champion classes.

153

UNDERSTANDING
THE DOG SHOW

To the novice, exhibiting a Bichon Havanese in the show ring may look easy but it usually takes a lot of hard work and devotion to do top winning at a show such as the prestigious Crufts, not to mention a little luck too!

The first concept that the canine novice learns when watching a dog show is that each breed first competes against members of its own breed. Once the judge has selected the best member of each breed, provided that the show is judged on a Group system, that chosen dog will compete with other dogs in its group. Finally the best of each group will compete for Best in Show and Reserve Best in Show.

The second concept that you must understand is that the dogs are not actually competing against one another. The judge compares each dog against the breed standard, which is a written description of the ideal specimen of the breed. Whilst some early breed standards were indeed based on specific dogs that were famous or popular, many dedicated enthusiasts say that a perfect specimen, described in the standard, has never been bred. Thus the 'perfect' dog never walked into a show ring, has never been bred and, to the woe of dog breeders around the globe, does not exist. Breeders attempt to get as close to this ideal

as possible, with every litter, but theoretically the 'perfect' dog is so elusive that it is impossible. (And if the 'perfect' dog were born, breeders and judges would never agree that it was indeed 'perfect.')

If you are interested in exploring dog shows, your best bet is to join your local breed club. These clubs often host both Championship and Open shows, and sometimes Match meetings and Special Events, all of which could be of interest, even if you are only an onlooker. Clubs also send out newsletters and some organise training days and seminars in order that people may learn more about their chosen breed. To locate the nearest breed club for you, contact The Kennel Club, the ruling body for the British dog world. The Kennel Club governs not only conformation shows but also working trials, obedience trials, agility trials and field trials. The Kennel Club furnishes the rules and regulations for all these events plus general dog registration and other basic requirements of dog ownership. Its annual show called the Crufts Dogs Show, held in Birmingham, is the largest bench show in England. Every year around 20,000 of the U.K.'s best dogs qualify to participate in this marvellous show which lasts four days.

The Kennel Club governs many different kinds of shows in Great Britain, Australia, South Africa and beyond. At the most competitive and prestigious of these shows, the Championship Shows, a dog can earn Challenge Certificates, and thereby become a Show Champion or a Champion. A dog must earn three Challenge Certificates under three different judges to earn the prefix of 'Sh Ch.' or 'Ch.' Note that some breeds must also qualify in a field trial in order to gain the title of full champion. Challenge Certificates are awarded to a very small percentage of the dogs competing, especially as dogs which are already Champions compete with others for these coveted CCs. The number of Challenge Certificates awarded in any one year is based upon the total number of dogs in each breed entered for competition. There three types of Championship Shows, an all-breed General Championship show for all Kennel Club recognised, a Group Championship Show, limited to breeds within one of the groups, and a Breed Show, usually confined to a single breed. The Kennel Club determines which breeds at which Championship Shows will have the opportunity to earn Challenge Certificates (or tickets). Serious exhibitors often will opt not to participate if the tickets are withheld at a particular show. This policy makes earning championships ever more difficult to accomplish.

Open Shows are generally less competitive and are frequently used as 'practice shows' for young dogs. There are hundreds of Open Shows each year.

FÉDÉRATION CYNOLOGIQUE INTERNATIONALE
Established in 1911, the Fédération Cynologique Internationale (FCI) represents the 'world kennel club.' This international body brings uniformity to the breeding, judging and showing of purebred dogs. Although the FCI originally included only four European nations: France, Holland, Austria and Belgium (which remains its headquarters), the organisation today embraces nations on six continents and recognises well over 300 breeds of purebred dog. There are three titles attainable through the FCI: the International Champion, which is the most prestigious; the International Beauty Champion, which is based on aptitude certificates in different countries; and the International Trial Champion, which is based on achievement in obedience trials in different countries. Quarantine laws in England and Australia prohibit most of their exhibitors from entering FCI shows. The rest of the Continent does participate in these impressive canine spectacles, the largest of which is the World Dog Show, hosted in a different country each year. FCI sponsors both national and international shows. The hosting country determines the judging system and breed standards are always based on the breed's country of origin.

INDEX

Page numbers in **boldface** indicate illustrations.

My Bichon Havanese

PUT YOUR PUPPY'S FIRST PICTURE HERE

Dog's Name _____

Date _____ Photographer _____